THE NORMANS

Text by
DAVID NICOLLE PHD.
Colour plates by
ANGUS McBRIDE

First published in Great Britain in 1987 by
Osprey Publishing, Elms Court, Chapel Way, Botley,
Oxford OX2 9LP, United Kingdom.
Email: *osprey@osprey-publishing.co.uk*
Also published as Elite 9 *The Normans*

ISBN 1 85532 944 1

Filmset in Great Britain
Printed through World Print Ltd, Hong Kong

FOR A CATALOGUE OF ALL BOOKS PUBLISHED BY
OSPREY MILITARY, AUTOMOTIVE AND AVIATION
PLEASE WRITE TO:

The Marketing Manager, Osprey Direct USA,
PO Box 130, Sterling Hts, MI 48311-0130
United States of America
Email: info@OspreyDirectUSA.com

The Marketing Manager, Osprey Direct UK,
PO Box 140, Wellingborough, Northants, NN8 4ZA,
United Kingdom
Email: info@OspreyDiret.co.uk

VISIT OSPREY'S WEBSITE AT:

http://www.osprey-publishing.co.uk

Dedication
For Chantal, who reminded me of an obligation.

FRONT COVER: The Bayeux Tapestry - 11th Century.
(By special permission of the City of Bayeux)
BACK COVER: Courtesy of David Nicolle.

The Norman Legacy

The importance of the Normans in British and European history is denigrated, or at least accepted only grudgingly, by the English-speaking world. It is as if the English still could not come to terms with defeat by an army of supposed Frenchmen at the battle of Hastings (1066). European scholars have generally taken a more objective view of the Normans and their spectacular two centuries of conquest. While the Anglo-Saxons created England, many would argue that the Normans at least began the creation of the United Kingdom of England, Wales, Scotland, the Channel Islands, the Isle of Man and, even to this day, part of Ireland.

The Norman contribution to French history is important, though less clear-cut; while the state they established in southern Italy and Sicily survived under successor dynasties until the unification of Italy in the 19th century. The last 'Norman state', that of the Principality of Antioch in northern Syria, has received far less attention. It was clearly not so important in world history; yet its rôle in the story of the Crusades was in many respects as central as that of the Kingdom of Jerusalem itself.

Who were the medieval Normans? Were they tamed Vikings or provincial Frenchmen? Xenophobic English historians have argued that they never were a distinct people; but the fact remains that the Normans themselves and many of their contemporaries believed in a *Gens Normannorum* ('the Norman people'). Ethnic origins are irrelevant: if a group think that they are a separate entity, then they are one—even if only for a limited period. These *Normanni* certainly cultivated a sense of identity and common characteristics which, in the case of the Normans, tended to be of a military and political type. Ferocity, boundless energy, cunning and a capacity for leadership were their heritage, to which modern scholars would add

'St. Michael, Captain of the Heavenly Host', and one of the warrior saints beloved of the Normans: from a Norman manuscript from Mont St. Michel, 980–1000. (Ms. 50, Bib.Munic., Avranches)

supreme adaptability and a simple piety. This sense of *Normannitas* (Normanness) survived into the 13th century, but was by then being submerged beneath new national identities which survive to this day— French, English, Scots and Irish. The situation in Italy was obviously different; while in Antioch, personal identity remained largely religious to the end.

In the early days similarities between the

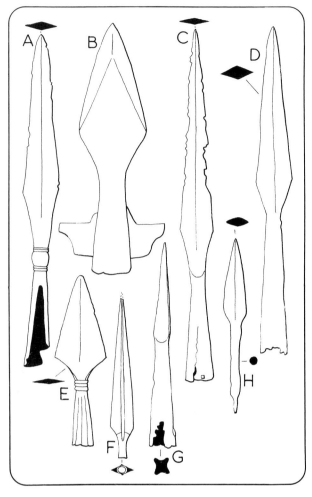

Spearheads of the Norman era: *A* = **English, 10th–12th C. (location unknown)**; *B* = **Northern French, 11th–12th C. (local Mus., St. Germain)**; *C* = **from Fornham, England, c. 1170 (Bury St. Edmunds Mus.)**; *D* = **from Cork, Ireland, 1250–1300 (Cork Public Mus.)**; *E* = **from Aldersgate, London, late 12th–13th C. (Guildhall Mus.)**; *F* = **from Atlit Castle, Israel (location unknown)**; *G* = **from Clough Castle, Ireland, 13th C. (location unknown)**; *H* = **from Dublin, 13th C. (Nat.Mus., Dublin)**

Normans and their Viking predecessors were clear enough. Amazing military successes resulted from careful planning, speed of movement, decisiveness, daring and sheer ruthlessness. Added to this was a strong business sense and an appreciation of the value of money. Yet it was the Normans' adaptability that set them apart from the Vikings. Both dominated their age militarily; but the Normans soon adopted Carolingian feudalism, cavalry warfare and castles to build archetypal feudal states in Normandy and England. They also adopted Christianity, and became the strong sword-arm of a reforming Church hierarchy.

In Italy they adopted advanced Byzantine or Islamic bureaucratic and financial structures, to build not only the most efficient but also perhaps the richest state in western Europe. In England they took over Anglo-Saxon political and legal institutions. By adding strong leadership and improved financial organisation they guided the kingdom towards that fusion of democracy and law, strong government and individual freedom that was to become England's main contribution to European history. To differing degrees similar processes occurred in Scotland and the other Celtic states.

A vital key to such successes, military and political, was the Normans' characteristic toleration. If obedience and taxation were forthcoming they generally left their subjects alone. In Italy and Sicily this resulted in one of the great flowerings of culture in European history. Elsewhere the result was relative stability in which economic, political and cultural advances could take place.

Arms, Armour and Tactics

The years during which the Normans dominated European warfare saw the final phase of the so-called 'age of mail', while their years of decline witnessed the beginnings of a transition to plate armour. Developments in tactics and horse-harness led to many changes in arms and armour, and were themselves influenced by these changes. In western Europe the most important development was the adoption of the couched lance, gripped firmly between the upper arm and the chest. With this new tactic came the high war-saddle with its protective pommel, raised and subsequently hip-hugging cantle, shock-absorbing breast strap, and straight-legged riding position. The latter feature, which enabled a rider to stand in his stirrups, probably had more to do with the use of a long broadsword than with the spear or lance. Before the adoption of a straight-legged riding position the sword was of less importance to a horseman than was a spear: with shorter stirrups an over-enthusiastic cut, particularly sideways, could easily lead to a fall.

The almost universal acceptance of these new ideas by the western European knightly class of the late 11th and early 12th centuries was a major feature of warfare in this period. An increasing use of archery, particularly of crossbows, by the infantry was an equally important development in the 12th century. In fact the crossbow was probably a more important stimulus in the readoption of plate armour than was the couched lance. It would, of course, have been strange if the 12th and early 13th centuries had not witnessed dramatic developments in the military field, as this period was very creative in most other aspects of culture.

Changes in armour could be summarised as follows. A mail hauberk remained the most common form of protection, apart from a shield, but it grew in size to include full-length sleeves with mail mittens and, for cavalry, to reach the knees. Padded garments were now clearly worn beneath hauberks, although they might always have been so worn. Shields increased in their variety of styles and sizes, but the old kite-shaped form probably remained the most common until about 1200. Swords became more slender and tapering, but in some parts of Arab-influenced southern Europe, including Norman Italy and Sicily, a broad non-tapering type of blade remained popular. The disappearance of right-angled lugs from beneath the spearhead accompanied the adoption of the couched lance. European lance blades became small and more pointed, clearly being designed to puncture armour or shields rather than cause wide wounds. Although the 'chicken and egg' problem is characteristic of the study of arms and armour, such changes in lance-blades must be associated with the couched lance, the large shield and the spread of plate armour.

The most dramatic changes were, however, seen in helmets. Throughout the 11th and early 12th centuries variations on a basic conical helmet, with or without a nasal and made from one piece of iron or from sections joined in different ways, were almost universal, though lower, round-topped helmets were also used in some regions. By the year 1200 the flat-topped 'great helm' had made its appearance, and would become both widespread and increasingly heavy during the 13th century. The stages of its early development can be charted in pictorial sources, beginning with the attachment of a visor to an ordinary conical helmet, or even with the steady broadening of a nasal. Flat-topped

Warrior with an oval shield, late 11th–early 12th centuries: a carved capital, *in situ* Ruquerville church, near Bayeux, Normandy.

helmets, far from being the technological aberration that some scholars have suggested, were a response to a horizontal threat to the face and neck from a couched lance, arrow or crossbow bolt. Obviously they were less effective against a downward blow from a sword or mace, which must, therefore, have been regarded as a lesser threat during this period.

Written sources indicate that some form of semi-rigid body defence was almost certainly known by 1200 but was, throughout western Europe, invisible beneath a mail hauberk and surcoat. Written evidence also suggests that small pieces of plate armour for the elbows and knees were adopted slightly earlier than the pictorial evidence would indicate.

The rôle of the Normans as transmitters of more advanced forms of armour from the East to the West seems to have been important. This would have

'The Betrayal'—marble candlestick made by Nicola d'Angelo and Pietro Vassalletto, c. 1170. (San Paolo fuori la Mura, Rome)

contrast, the rigid face mask which rapidly developed into the great helm may have been an internal European development.

The precise origins of most medieval tactical innovations remain a matter of debate, but the rôle of the Normans in the dissemination of new ideas is clear. The couched lance, the long kite-shaped shield and the small but manoeuvrable cavalry formation using this weaponry were typical of the 11th- and 12th-century Normans, yet they were probably first developed in mid-10th-century Byzantium. The primary duty of heavy cavalry was to break an enemy formation by controlled charges; but, whereas in Byzantium lancers occupied only the flanks of such formations, leaving the initial collision to men with swords or maces, the Normans and other Westerners all seem to have wielded lances. The larger shield associated with the couched lance was worn rather than held, its weight being carried by the shoulder as well as the arm. This meant that it could hardly be moved, and was more akin to a piece of armour. It protected a rider's left side, but also limited his movement in the saddle. The newly adopted straight-legged riding position similarly inhibited a horseman's movement. Together they would, by the 13th century, virtually force a European cavalryman to use his lance in the couched style and no other.

Although the couched lance technique may not have been invented in western Europe, it was adopted there with greater enthusiasm than elsewhere, for both social and military reasons. This was particularly true of northern France, Normandy and Anglo-Norman England. In Europe the fully armoured cavalryman soon became the 'knight' of the High Middle Ages, and was already more than just a warrior. He was becoming part of an exclusive military caste whose code of conduct often governed his mode of combat. A knight should fight a knight, both being similarly equipped. They could attack one another in a style approved by class and custom, seeking no 'unfair' advantage and craving 'honour' above mere victory.

This might not yet have been the case in the 11th century, but features of the tournament and its associated cult of Courtly Love were already appearing. While William the Conqueror's horsemen in the *Bayeux Tapestry* could revert to more old-fashioned ways of using their spears after failing to

been particularly true of those in southern Italy, Sicily, Byzantine mercenary service or the Crusader Principality of Antioch. It is now clear that medieval Byzantine and Muslim warriors were not always as lightly armed as was once thought. Their armours included a padded and cloth-covered mail hauberk or jerkin known in the Middle East as a *kazhagand*. This reached western Europe at the end of the 11th century and was called a *jazerant*. It is also possible that the iron or hardened leather lamellar cuirass of the Middle East and Balkans played a part in the development of the western European coat-of-plates or of its cruder predecessors. The separate mail aventail which, attached to the rim of a helmet, largely replaced a mail coif in the late 13th century, was almost certainly of Eastern origin. Horse-armour was, with a few debatable exceptions, unknown in early medieval Europe, but reappeared in the 12th century; horse-armour had, however, never been abandoned by the Byzantines or their Turkish and Muslim foes. In

break the Anglo-Saxon shield-wall at Hastings, the slightly later author of the *Song of Roland* seemed to be writing a triumph for the new knight and his characteristic weapon.

The situation was somewhat different when a Norman (or indeed any other western European) knight was fighting a non-Western foe. In many cases his tactics and equipment proved devastatingly effective. In others he seemed unable to reach his opponent or even to protect himself. Under such circumstances Western knights appear to have been more successful when copying the controlled tactics and small formations invented by the Byzantines, particularly when their charges were launched against static foes. Against a moving and mounted target they were rarely successful. A horse, however well trained, will not normally gallop right into an obstacle, human or otherwise, unless it can see a way around; but a lance enables a rider to strike a target as he passes and at a range of some feet. Except when couched, the lance can also be thrust at a target while the horse is stationary. When couched, however, a lance can only be used effectively against an impassable obstacle such as a rank of infantrymen if the horse is trained to push. The high saddle, the rigid riding position, and the fact that the lance was held behind its point of balance to give greater reach, in addition to being locked beneath the rider's upper arm, may all

Huntsman dressed in mail and helmet, carrying bow—a 12th-century carving *in situ*, north door, La Martorana, Palermo.

indicate that such a pushing technique holds the secret of many early Norman cavalry successes. Perhaps the Papal infantry at Civitate in 1053, the Siculo-Muslims at Enna in 1061, the Anglo-Saxons at Hastings in 1066 and their descendants in Byzantine service at Durres (Durazzo) in 1081 were actually jostled rather than smashed into defeat.

The situation in cavalry-versus-cavalry combat was obviously not the same. After an initial charge the struggle almost inevitably dissolved into a mêlée if one side did not immediately flee. Here the couched lance seemed to provide no obvious advantage, yet men are constantly recorded as being unhorsed, often by lance thrusts, in circumstances where only a rider's arm could give power to his blow. There are, in fact, clear references to lances being used in a variety of ways during the mêlée. The high saddle and long stirrup associated with the couched lance also made it difficult for dismounted men to remount. Perhaps the continued employment of lighter cavalry—serjeants in Europe, both these and more specialised Turcopoles in Crusader Syria—reflected the limitations of a fully armoured knight in a mêlée.

Only recently have historians used psychological techniques, developed during and after the Second World War, to probe the probable stresses faced by men and animals in pre-industrial warfare. What, for example, was the reality of medieval 'cavalry shock' tactics against disciplined or at least determined infantry? Were infantry more afraid of horses or of the men riding them? Did cavalry fear archers more or less than they feared other cavalry? What happened when charging cavalry met disciplined infantry in ranks, and at what speed did they come into contact? What effect did the impact have on any second rank of cavalry or on the further ranks of infantry? What happened when two forces of cavalry on the move met head-on, and how closely packed were such units when they collided? How, in fact, did cavalry 'pass through' other cavalry, or 'ride down' infantry? Clearly the results of combat were intended to be more predictable than the results of a suicidal accident. Unfortunately, medieval illustrations of battle often portray what looks like the split-second prior to a violent encounter rather than realistic combat. This is often true even where knights are shown jousting with couched lances. In a real joust the horses pass by one another, after which they continue until they either stop or are stopped. Such a state of affairs could only be duplicated on the battlefield if two forces of cavalry were in single ranks in reasonably open order, and had agreed on the identity of their personal opponents beforehand—a most unlikely occurrence, even if it suited the ideal of chivalric warfare perfectly! Many such questions remain unanswered, particularly in the Norman period.

The Normans in Normandy

The region that became Normandy was not a new creation of the Normans. It was approximately the same as the old church province of Rouen and, lacking natural frontiers, was little more than an administrative unit agreed upon by the Norman duke and the French king. Its population had been essentially Gallo-Roman with a small Frankish (Germanic) addition. A substantial number of Scandinavians (Vikings) had settled, but they were divided between small colonies in Upper (eastern) Normandy and larger colonies in Lower (western) Normandy. Scandinavian colonisation began at the end of the 9th century; but in 911 Rollo, a leader of the Seine valley settlers, forced Charles III of France to recognise his occupation of part of Upper

Normandy, probably in return for his accepting Christianity and giving military aid to the French monarch. This Treaty of St. Clair-sur-Epte is shrouded in legend; but it is clear that by 923 Rollo had won control over the other Scandinavian settlers in Lower Normandy. His successors pushed back the frontier with Brittany and made Rouen into a flourishing mercantile city, in close contact with Scandinavia and the Viking-ruled parts of northern England.

Thereafter, until William the Bastard's crushing victory at Val-ès-Dunes in 1047, Norman history centred upon the struggle of successive dukes to unite Normandy and dominate its warlike aristocracy. Until the early 11th century the Normans were still Viking in character, welcoming Scandinavian raiding fleets as allies. On the other hand one important Viking institution, the democratic assembly or *thing*, was never seen among the Normans. Early Normandy was also militarily weak compared to its neighbours, Norman forces

Although crudely executed, weathered by the centuries, and photographed in shadow, these two carvings of Anglo-Norman warriors, *c.* 1180, from the south door of St. Mary's Barfraston church in Kent can still be seen to show the horseman with his lance in the couched position, and the knight on foot with a conical nasal helm, a split hauberk, and a 'kite' shield with the top edge 'cut off' straight.

being smaller than those of Anjou as well as having inferior discipline.

Feudalism

As the feudalisation of Normandy progressed, so Norman strength grew. Feudalism has often been described in misleadingly simplified terms. Essentially, however, it was a means of unifying a state by binding together ruler and ruled, king with duke, local lord with humble knight, through solemn oaths of vassalage, fealty or homage. This was considered an 'honourable' arrangement, and it formed a contract under which the strong agreed to defend the weak, the weak to support the strong. The more favoured a vassal, the more likely he was to be awarded a piece of land or *fief*, plus its inhabitants. This he held as the tenant of his lord. Such an estate was to help a vassal, usually a knight, to afford the increasingly expensive military equipment of the day. This was the archetypal *fief de haubert*—the hauberk being a mail shirt which

'The Death of Absalom', in a painted Bible probably made in Winchester, Hampshire, *c.* 1150–75. Note the clearly painted details: the high saddle with twin girths; the hauberks with mittens and ventails or coifs; the round-topped helmet (left) with a nasal and with painted motifs; the so-called 'Phrygian cap' version of the nasal helmet (centre), with its forward-tilting shape perhaps indicating extra thickness of metal at the front; and the kite shield painted in chevrons. Several other scenes from the life of David on this same page all show knights in either round-topped or 'Phrygian cap'-shaped helmets; other shield patterns include diagonal 'bends' and two-colour chequers set diamond-fashion on the shield. (Pierpont Morgan Library, M.619 verso, New York)

'Tristan fights Morhaut': a painted marriage chest, probably Breton, of 1150–70. (Cathedral Treasury, Vannes)

supposedly distinguished an élite armoured cavalryman from the rest of the army. The fief also freed the warrior from manual work so that he could concentrate on his military skills.

Medieval terminology is notoriously imprecise, but it does seem that the *milites* were true vassals, though not necessarily holding land, while the *stipendiarii* swore lesser oaths and fought primarily for pay. Each could, however, be regarded as an early form of knight. Comparable bonds linked the peasants with the enfiefed vassal, but were decreasingly 'honourable', which in turn reflected the declining military status of the general peasant levy. Not that foot soldiers as such were disappearing from the scene. In fact infantry seem to have grown more specialised, and were no longer simply drawn from an untrained peasantry. Deep-rooted as Norman feudalism was by the mid-11th century, it was never as neat as the system imposed upon England after 1066. One Norman peculiarity was the *vavasseur*, an unclear military status and form of land tenure between knight and peasant which was probably a left-over from pre-feudal times.

Duke, lords and church

In many parts of Europe the growing effectiveness of the military class led to private war and near-anarchy, but in Normandy it was accompanied by a growth in the power of the duke. This was not a smooth process, as ducal authority—particularly over castle-building—suffered a setback in the 1030s and 1040s. A breakthrough came in the reign of Duke William—later William the Conqueror—before his invasion of England in 1066. At first William co-operated with his military aristocracy; then in 1047, he crushed those who still defied him in the decisive battle of Val-ès-Dunes. During the following years the duke's government was aggressive, warlike and much to the taste of his knights and nobles. He was, in fact, a fine general, calm but decisive and well able to win the respect of ordinary soldiers. William's exceptional organisational ability was well illustrated in his gathering of an army and a fleet in 1066. The duke's own large estates (*domain*) enabled him to enfief and enrich loyal supporters, who were then placed in command of key castles and forces. Duke William did not, however, have such control over castle-building, and so had to take a more persuasive, co-operative line with his barons. Yet he did win the right to enter any castle, so stopping local lords from falsely seizing additional fortifications in his name. Neither were economic measures ignored, the development of William's favourite city of Caen being encouraged in an effort to strengthen ducal authority in Lower Normandy.

Powerful as William might have grown by 1066, the duke still had to consult his barons and win their sometimes grudging support for his great invasion of England. Diplomatic preparations were also vital. Duke William remained a vassal of France, virtually independent though he now seemed. Yet he convinced most European rulers of his right to the English crown, and above all he won Papal support, symbolised by a banner which was flown at Hastings.

The warlike aristocracy which Duke William came to dominate was a new class of new men compared to the old aristocracy of France. These latter often claimed descent from Carolingian times, but few Norman families could trace their ancestry back before 1010. The military class had also bred with remarkable speed. Most knights remained poor and land-hungry, land-hunger being simply a matter of survival, and by 1066 Normandy had been exporting warriors for more than a generation.

The alliance between Duke William and the Papacy reflected a long-standing co-operation between the Norman leadership and the Church. The Church helped unify Normandy; many ecclesiastical leaders came from the Norman aristocracy, while others were retired warriors. The secular aristocracy enthusiastically founded monasteries, many of which then owed military service for their lands. In fact it seems as if many of the earliest landed knights were linked to such abbeys, particularly those near exposed frontiers. Not that there was yet any great social distinction between landed and landless knights. Knighthood itself held little status, and merely indicated that a man was a professional warrior. He often appeared as a mere statistic, as in a pre-1066 charter of the Abbey of St. Père de Chartres which described one village as having 'a church, land for three plough teams, twelve peasants, five free knights and a mill'. Nor did knighthood yet involve much pomp or display: rather, it consisted of hard training and harder knocks.

Tactics

Cavalry training was undertaken in groups of five to ten. Standards of discipline were clearly higher than most critics of medieval warfare have allowed, and the same was probably true of command and control at this basic unit level. It might also be fair to say that medieval generalship was as good—or as inadequate—as in any other age.

The basic fighting unit was the *conroi* of 20 to 30 men in two or three ranks. This would have been identified by its own small spear-mounted flag or *gonfanon*. While shield devices were probably only decorative at this time, flags were essential for command and control. The evidence suggests that the Norman *conroi*, or the larger *bataille* to which it contributed, was well able to make controlled charges, to wheel, to turn, and even to retreat in 'feigned flight'—a difficult manoeuvre demanding discipline and adequate signalling procedures.

The whole question of the feigned retreat by 11th-century Norman cavalry is still hotly debated.

It seems to have been employed against the French at St. Aubin in 1053 and against the Sicilian Arabs at Messina in 1060. The Normans might have learned it from their Breton neighbours, or from men returning from service in southern Italy or Spain. Breton cavalry seem to have known of the feigned retreat even in the 10th century, and it is worth noting that the Breton left wing at Hastings was the first part of Duke William's army apparently to retreat. This is normally considered

Sword-hilts of the Norman era: *A* = **Italian, 11th C.? (location unknown);** *B* = **probably Continental European, 11th–12th C. (Bunratty Castle, Co. Clare, Ireland);** *C* = **probably English, 13th C. (Wallace Coll., London);** *D* = **French, blade inscribed GICELINMEFECIT—'Giselin made me'—***c.* **1130–70 (private coll.);** *E* = **hilt and scabbard of the Ceremonial Imperial Sword of the Holy Roman Empire, prob. made Sicily,** *c.* **1220 (Kunsthist.Mus., Vienna);** *F* = **French,** *c.* **1150–75 (Coll. P-R. Royer, Paris);** *G* = **enamelled pommel of sword of Peter of Dreux, prob. captured at Mansurah, 1250, subsequently purchased in Damascus (Met.Mus. of Art, New York);** *H* = **pommel of Syrian manufacture for a European owner, 13th C. (Met.Mus. of Art, New York)**

Sharpening a sword: detail from an Anglo-Norman manuscript of *c.* 1150. (*Eadwine Psalter*, **Ms.R.17.1, Trinity College Lib., Cambridge**)

to have been a genuine flight, whereas the second retreat by the duke's own men is widely regarded as a feigned flight. Literary descriptions of the battle of Hastings also concentrate on swords rather than spears: perhaps the latter were soon broken against Saxon shields, or had been hurled at the foe. Cavalry training certainly included the throwing of javelins from horseback.

In wider strategic terms the supposedly impetuous Normans were notably cautious in warfare, often adopting a patient wait-and-see attitude. Careful reconnaissance was normal, and winter campaigns common. On the other hand battles involving only cavalry were rare, at least in France. The rôle of infantry remained important, and 11th-century knights were both trained and willing to fight on foot. References to *milites pedites*—'foot-knights'—are, however, few in relation to the total of ordinary *milites*.

We do not know how such men were armed, but archery was certainly important among the Normans, Duke William himself being a renowned bowman. Their conquest of England led to a great increase in the use of the bow in the British Isles. Two distinct classes of archers are shown on the Bayeux Tapestry, those in the main picture being well dressed or even armoured, while those in the lower panel are a ragged band. Perhaps the former are professionals, the latter representatives of a general levy or *arrière ban*—a rarely used and shadowy remnant of the old Germanic levy of all free men. At the end of the Bayeux Tapestry one Norman archer pursues the defeated Saxons on horseback. He wears spurs; and while this might be

an artistic error, it has been used as evidence either for the unlikely existence of Norman horse-archers, or to indicate that professional bowmen were mobile mounted infantry. The Norman archers at Hastings were skilled and disciplined enough to drop flights of arrows on their foes in a form of zone-shooting normally associated with Byzantines or Turks. It is even possible that some of the shorter bows in the Bayeux Tapestry were of southern European composite construction: perhaps these were used by mercenaries enrolled by Duke William? Other evidence suggests that crossbows were employed, though none are illustrated on the Tapestry. They were clearly already known in France, and would become common among the Normans soon afterwards.

*   *   *

By the end of the 10th century the increasing power of the military aristocracy had already given rise to the Peace of God movement in southern and central France. In this the Church and common people tried to curb the violence of lesser barons and knights. Local rulers often supported the movement, as they had an interest in stability if not in actual peace. Duke Richard II of Normandy at first rejected the Peace of God, trusting in his own ability to keep the peace. Near-anarchy followed his death, and Duke William was happy to proclaim his own Truce of God in 1047, the year of Val-ès-Dunes. This truce laid down the days when fighting was banned and also listed those people who could not be harmed in 'private warfare'. The duke himself and his armies were, of course, exempt from such restrictions.

As a virtually independent prince, the duke of Normandy had political relationships with neighbouring rulers, the most important of whom was his nominal suzerain, the king of France. After defeating the last French attempt to destroy the duchy in 987 the Norman dukes followed a relatively consistent policy of support for the French crown. Tensions remained, and even as late as 1054 and 1058 the king invaded. Anjou and Flanders were, however, normally the main threats to Normandy.

Norman relations with Anglo-Saxon England were more straightforward. In the year 1000 an Anglo-Saxon fleet may even have attacked western Normandy to forestall Viking raiders based there;

but as Normandy became Christian in religion and French in speech, so its dukes found a common interest with the rulers of southern Britain in closing the English Channel to Viking fleets. This alliance broke up when the Normans supported Edward and the House of Wessex against Cnut of Denmark in their struggle for the English throne. When Edward (the Confessor) returned from exile in Normandy to take the English crown he was, understandably, pro-Norman in his sympathies. As a man of southern England, Edward feared the Scandinavian threat and knew that a Norman succession after his death would finally close the Channel to the Vikings. The paucity and tendentious character of surviving evidence also means that Duke William's claim to the English throne should perhaps be given more credibility than it normally is.

The Norman duke's comparable fear of Scandinavian intervention contributed to William's alliance with his erstwhile rivals in Flanders in 1066.

Other perennial victims of Viking raiders had been the Channel Islands or Îles Normandes. These are not, nor have they ever been, part of England; nor, contrary to popular opinion, were they part of the duchy of Normandy in 1066. The islands were instead a personal dependency of Duke William, as were the Counties of Brittany and Maine. Like these areas, they contributed men and ships to the great expedition of 1066.

Many Norman warriors, administrators and churchmen had served in England under Edward the Confessor. Some were responsible for reorganising English defences along the Welsh borders around 1055, though their attempts to introduce Norman-French styles of cavalry ultimately failed in battle. Not until 1066 was English military tradition really changed.

Siege of Jerusalem 'portrayed upon a tile' (Ezek.4.1.), showing wheeled battering rams, and some of the earlier representations of crossbows; from a manuscript from Auxerre, *c.* 1000. (*Commentaries of Hayman on Ezekiel*, Ms.Lat.12302, Bib.Nat., Paris)

The central motte of Gisors Castle; the circular wall was built in the 11th century, the tall watchtower being added at the end of the 12th century.

The Norman conquest of England was perhaps the single most dramatic event in British history, but it was less important in the history of Normandy itself. During the early post-Conquest years the wealth and strength of England helped the dukes strengthen their position. This can be seen in the *Consuetudines* of 1091, which gave the ruler greater control over castle-building as well as the right to occupy any fortification whenever he wanted to. It stated that a man might not attack an enemy if this foe was on his way to or from the duke's court or army. Pilgrims and merchants were similarly protected. Pillaging was banned, as was the burning of houses and mills and damage to agricultural tools. Such efforts to control endemic violence were limited to what was practically possible, but this Norman Peace did go beyond the earlier Peace of God by banning fighting on Wednesdays and Monday mornings. . .

As before, the development of government power went in fits and starts. After William the Conqueror died in 1087 his realm was divided between William II, who became King of England, and Robert 'Curthose', who ruled Normandy somewhat ineffectively. The duchy consequently fell into anarchy, with the aristocracy recovering much of its lost independence. Not until 1106 were the two areas reunited under Henry I, who went on to demolish most of the unauthorised 'adulterine' castles recently erected.

Meanwhile the status of the knights continued to rise, until, by the mid-12th century, they had become a true minor aristocracy. With this went the development of heraldry and the passing on of motifs—though not as yet true coats-of-arms—from father to son. This preceded the adoption of closed helmets which hid the wearer's face, and was probably unconnected with it. The first certain reference to undoubted Norman heraldry was in 1127, when Henry I knighted his son-in-law Geoffrey of Anjou and gave him the badge of gold lions on a blue ground. A lion might already have been Henry's own badge. Two lions were used by Henry II, and two lions or leopards on red remain the arms of Normandy to this day. A third beast was subsequently added by Richard I to distinguish the arms of England. King Stephen is sometimes credited with arms of three gold centaurs on red: this was probably a later invention, though he might have had a centaur or 'sagittary' as a badge.

The military demands made upon knights in Normandy were actually less than those seen in Anglo-Norman England; but whereas the rural knights of England were largely demilitarised in the late Norman and Angevin periods, the knights of Normandy remained a warrior class for longer. In England a tax called *scutage* (shield money) was paid in preference to military service, and the idea eventually spread to Normandy, where it was adopted earlier than in the rest of France.

Shaken by a rebellion in 1173–74, Henry II set about regularising the military situation. The first result was the Assize of Northampton (1176) which investigated the duties of castle guard in England. Four years later these were reformed, and in the same year the Ordnance of Le Mans did the same for the king's French provinces. In 1181 the Assize of Arms sorted out the question of personal and government weaponry, as well as prohibiting the export of military stores and equipment. These Assizes stated that a knight should have at least a hauberk, helmet, shield and lance, an ordinary freeman a smaller mail *haubergeon*, an iron cap and a lance. The urban burgess class was permitted a padded gambeson as armour, an iron cap and a lance but no more. Military equipment was, in fact, growing more expensive, and the best was consequently limited to a professional élite. In 1080 a mail hauberk cost 100 *sous*, from two to five times as much as a horse. A horse itself was worth five times as much as a bull, and by the 13th century a war-horse or *destrier* was no less than seven times as valuable as an ordinary horse. The best *destriers* came from Spain, northern Italy or Sicily.

One way to obtain this expensive equipment was to win it in a tournament; but Henry II had banned tournaments in England. Those who sought fame, fortune and adventure in this field had to travel to France, Flanders, Burgundy or Champagne. The warrior class was inevitably becoming stratified between knights, *bachelers*, *pueri*, *armigeri* (squires), *vavassors*, *serviens*, serjeants and others. By 1133 *vavassor* service in Normandy was expected only of men holding 50 to 60 acres, and they were later regarded as being worth from one quarter to one half of a full knight. The exact meaning of *bacheler* is still uncertain, but it probably referred to youthful enthusiasm and perhaps inexperience rather than to a strict military status.

One group of warriors who were clearly rising in importance were the mercenaries. They proved themselves not only to be better trained and equipped than most feudal warriors, but also more reliable. Various groups are recorded, including the highly respected Brabançons from present-day Belgium, and the fearsome Cottereaux and Routiers. The Brabançons appear mostly to have been *serjeants*, probably crossbowmen and spearmen of urban burgess background led by knights; but by 1202 they and other Flemish mercenaries included fully armoured cavalry on armoured horses. The Cottereaux may have been infantry of lower class or even outlaw origins, the Routiers perhaps being horsemen. Nevertheless, crossbowmen remained the mercenaries most in demand through this period. Mercenaries were employed not only for major campaigns but also to garrison castles. Aragonese from northern Spain are recorded under Henry II, while Richard I apparently introduced a few Muslim troops, either enslaved PoWs from the Crusader States or more probably men from Norman Sicily. (A relic of their brief service in Normandy might have been the two 'Turkish bows' of presumed composite construction listed among William Marshal's effects in 1246.) After Normandy and Anjou were lost to the French, men from these areas were still recruited as mercenaries by King John of England, who particularly welcomed skilled engineers.

A third group of warriors were the men from various vassal states. Some Welsh and Scottish contingents could be seen in this light, while troops from Brittany and Maine were clearly vassals. Even as late as 1120 Bretons were regarded as supreme cavalry but far less effective on foot. In the battle of Tinchebrai (1106) all of Henry I's army dismounted except the men of Brittany and Maine. At Lincoln (1141) the Bretons similarly refused to fight on foot. During the 12th century, however, the government, the administration and to a lesser extent the military styles of Brittany were remoulded in the Norman image, and traditional Celtic systems finally disappeared.

Norman warfare became more organised and sophisticated during the later 11th and 12th centuries, but there were few fundamental changes. Sieges were central features of almost all conflicts and most battles resulted from attempts to relieve a garrison. Battles were also regarded as unpredictable and potentially disastrous, so that set-piece

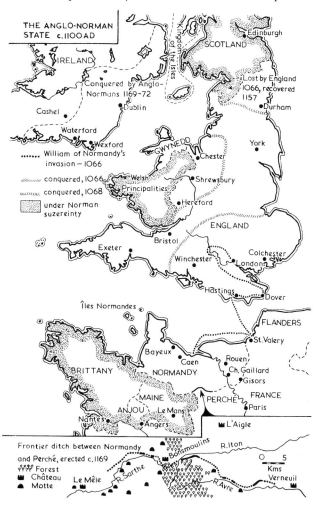

THE ANGLO-NORMAN STATE c.1100 AD

confrontations tended to be a last resort or a result of miscalculation. In fact many battles were avoided by truces or negotiations or by one side backing down. Unnecessary bloodshed within the military élite was similarly avoided. Knights disliked fighting their previous comrades, while even humbler infantry were often able to restrain knightly aggression against their fellows.

When open battle did take place it was clearly common for much of an army, including the knights, to fight on foot. At Alençon in 1118 an Angevin force of knights, followed by archers and other infantrymen, charged a Norman force of mixed cavalry and infantry. It seems as if the Angevin knights had dismounted and their archers were clearly very effective against the Normans' horses. At Brémule in 1119 a French cavalry charge was broken by Henry I's dismounted army, archers or crossbowmen again playing a vital part. At Bourgthéroulde in 1124 a force of rebel aristocrats on horseback charged a small unit of Henry's household troops. The latter had placed their archers in front with dismounted knights to support them, while another section of knights remained mounted and ready for a counter-charge. A smaller force of mounted archers were sent forward on the left to shoot at the enemy's unshielded right side, though they probably dismounted to use their bows. The result was a complete victory for these more professional household troops and archers.

When knights were fighting in their most characteristic manner as cavalry they still operated in small, closely-packed *conroi* units. The habit of wrapping a horse's breast-strap around the rear of its saddle showed that so-called 'shock tactics' with the couched lance were even more important than before. Similarly, the participation of unarmoured cavalry decreased dramatically. The classic *tourney* or tournament of the 12th century was still very like real cavalry warfare, with *conrois* of knights fighting in a mêlée. This was certainly not a free-for-all, as it involved manoeuvring by cavalry units and sometimes even the involvement of infantry, who assaulted any broken *conrois* in the flanks.

Norman infantry were not as yet organised in such recognisable units as were the cavalry—yet they were no rabble. Where possible they protected their flanks with natural obstacles such as rivers,

Exterior and interior of Chambois Castle. Unlike some Norman square keeps in England, this castle near the southern frontier of Normandy was clearly built with strength, rather than comfort in mind.

woods, hills or marshes. In open country round or rectangular formations were adopted, the shape being a matter of local tradition. At Rouen in 1174 a defensive ditch had to be filled so that a formation of infantrymen 200 wide could advance; they seem to have totalled 5,000 to 6,000 men in three corps 12 ranks deep. Light infantry with bows, spears or javelins reappeared in certain areas; their rôle was skirmishing, or protecting the flanks of the main force. Sometimes they acted as almost autonomous units.

Improvements in crossbow design were a vital feature of warfare in the 11th to 13th centuries. This weapon became very popular in the Norman areas from the reign of Henry I onwards. Compared with simple European handbows, crossbows were easy to shoot accurately, had more range, a flatter trajectory and considerably greater penetrating power. Their only disadvantage was in loading time. Even this was more characteristic of later and more powerful crossbows, which had to be 'spanned' by using a windlass or crank: earlier types were basically spanned manually. Lock mechanisms were at first all of wood, but some parts were soon being made of horn, with a still unsprung trigger of iron. The loading stirrup fastened with sinew or rope appeared late in the 11th century, a belt with a loading hook some time in the late 12th. Early crossbows were also large and heavy. The actual string still had to be pulled back up to 90cm, whereas 15th-century steel crossbows only had a draw of some 20cm. The incorporation of composite bows of mixed horn, wood, whalebone and sinew made for a smaller yet more powerful weapon. This was almost certainly a result of experience in southern Italy, Sicily or the Middle East.

Normandy had few naturally defensible frontiers; defence was consequently organised in depth. Walled towns like Verneuil, Tillières and Nonancourt along the River Avre were created primarily as defensive bases. Elsewhere numerous castles, strongly garrisoned and fully supplied, overlooked fords and other vulnerable points.

To the south the County of Anjou had been growing both in size and power. It posed a direct threat to Normandy whenever its count was in collusion with the French king. A marriage alliance between Normandy and Anjou seemed to solve this problem, although it ultimately led to an Angevin

The Citadel of Caen, whose walls were built by William the Conqueror in 1060.

takeover of the entire Norman realm. The process began on the death of Henry I. Civil war then raged between the supporters of his daughter Matilda, wife of Geoffrey of Anjou, and his nephew Count Stephen of Boulogne. The Angevin takeover started with Geoffrey's conquest of Normandy in 1144. Here he restored the powers of the duke, while remodelling the administration of Anjou along superior Norman lines. After Geoffrey's death in 1151 his son Henry (already made duke of Normandy) inherited both Maine and Anjou, acquired Aquitaine by marriage and, when Stephen died in 1154, became king of England as Henry II.

Now an Angevin empire stretched from Scotland to the Spanish frontier, and Normandy was the linchpin of this rambling realm. Under Henry II, Richard I and John links between England and Normandy were again strengthened. The ducal estates were regrouped as *bailiwicks* around important fortresses. Considerable military power was then placed in the hands of the *seneschals* of Normandy, a vital post given only to the ablest and most loyal of the king's supporters.

Not surprisingly, these developments alarmed the French king whose territories were now effectively, if not legally, much smaller than those of the Angevin dynasty. A new king of France, the clever and ruthless Philip, was dedicated to

'Guards at the Holy Sepulchre': copper alloy plaque, English, c. 1140-50. (Burrell Coll., Glasgow)

smashing Angevin power. His most obvious target was Normandy, an area which also isolated Paris from the Channel. Disputes about the possession of

The so-called Exchequer House within Caen Citadel, with the moat of the destroyed keep in the foreground. The building dates from Henry I's reign early in the 12th century, and was the great hall of the ducal palace.

he Vexin area in the Seine valley were serious in hemselves, but they also led to the final showdown. Richard I, known as the Lionhearted, defended Normandy successfully, though he might also have quandered his military and financial resources. His brother John inherited a far more difficult situation. Angevin power was scattered across an enormous mpire. Nor was John as respected by the Norman warrior class as his Crusading brother had been. The aristocracy of Normandy was also attracted by the increasingly brilliant culture of Paris, with its cult of chivalry, poetry and Courtly Love. Many till resented the Angevin takeover, and John found imself deserted by some leading barons. The angevin cause also suffered from the brutality of oth Richard's and John's mercenaries, particularly as much of the fighting took place on Norman oil. The French king was even able to use the Norman duke's right to enter castles by claiming nat he, as the duke's legitimate sovereign, should lso be permitted to enter any fortress he wished. he war dragged on sporadically until, in 1202, Philip launched a series of major campaigns. Brittany, part of Poitou, Touraine, Anjou, Maine nd finally, in the spring of 1204, Normandy itself ll.

The area would later again be dominated by the English during the Hundred Years War but, in 1204, one could say that for the first time in over 300 years Normandy had returned to the French fold. The consequences were less clear-cut for those involved. Many Anglo-Norman barons held lands on both sides of the Channel. Some did homage to both kings, but most remained in England. Normandy thus lost the bulk of its leading aristocracy and was quite easily absorbed into France. Nevertheless, Norman knights still sought employment in the remaining Angevin areas for many years.

The Normans in Britain and Ireland

In Normandy the years following 1066 saw a steady development of existing military styles, but in Britain they witnessed a military revolution. Duke

Château Gaillard overlooking the River Seine, built in 1196 by Richard I to defend Normandy from the French king.

William's invasion and the conquest of England were among the most astonishing feats of medieval arms, but the expedition was not a solely Norman affair. It attracted volunteers from all over France and beyond, many of whom subsequently settled in England. The planning was not particularly detailed, but the duke's strategy showed a real grasp of the geopolitical situation. William was clearly also capable of seizing an opportunity when it was offered.

Harold and his army were lured into an exhausting march south and then into a premature defensive battle. William's army then demonstrated—not without difficulty—the superiority of Norman-French mixed cavalry and infantry tactics over the Germanic-Scandinavian infantry traditions of the Anglo-Saxons. Clearly the couched lance was still being evolved, for spears were used in various other ways at Hastings. The throwing of such weapons was rare, but downward thrusts and other techniques were common. Most evidence relies on the Bayeux Tapestry, which may have been made, if not actually designed, by English seamstresses. The Tapestry might, in fact, be a more reliable representation of Anglo-Saxon than of Norman warriors.

The degree of continuity in English military systems after 1066 is still debated, but the military organisation of Anglo-Norman England was not uniform. Cavalry, for example, were drawn from more than just the ranks of the land-holding knightly class. Nor was the imposition of feudalism the same in all areas. Military burdens were unevenly spread, falling hardest on the earliest areas to be conquered. At first landless 'household' knights were the most immediately available force. Only after the conquest was secure were most knights settled on the land and given *fees* or fiefs. Even as late as the mid-12th century landless knights were a common feature of vulnerable frontier zones.

One of the most noticeable changes in the English military system was a steady emigration by the old Anglo-Saxon military élite, particularly by the generation following that defeated at Hastings. Younger warriors saw little hope of advancement in an England dominated by their conquerors. Although resistance had crumbled these men remained a threat to Norman security, and so their departure was welcomed by William the Conqueror and his son, William II. Some Anglo-Saxons left in the late 1060s, mostly to Denmark, and this emigration continued through the '70s and '80s. Large numbers moved on from Scandinavia in the wake of the famous Varangians, through Russia and down to Constantinople. Here the English became a major, perhaps even the main, element within the Byzantine Emperor's Guard. It has recently been suggested that one large group sailed directly to the eastern Mediterranean under Earl Sigurd in around 1075. The bulk then refused to serve as mere guardsmen and were sent northwards to retake the lost Byzantine province of Cherson in the Crimea. Here they are supposed to have merged with a Goth community surviving from the great age of Germanic migrations and, according to legend, to have created another *Nova Anglia* (New England) in southern Russia!

Back in Britain the departure of the old aristocracy did not mean the demilitarisation of the Anglo-Saxons as a whole. The military power of England was large, from 5,000 to 7,000 men if necessary, and the Normans made good use of it. English infantry often needed training by Norman professionals, particularly when called upon to fight against cavalry, but they seem to have been quick to learn. It was here that the strongest military continuity between Anglo-Saxon and Norman times can be seen. The rank-and-file of Anglo-Norman armies was of mixed origins, including men of noble blood, assimilated Englishmen and adventurers from many parts.

The Norman conquest raised the prestige of the bow as a war weapon and by the 12th century it had become perhaps the most effective tool in the defence of northern England against Scottish raiders. English influence on cavalry seems unlikely. The fact that the Anglo-Saxon word *cniht* (knight) was adopted in preference to the French *chevalier* as the term for a professional horse-warrior probably reflected the Anglicisation of the Norman élite rather than any direct military influence. The cultural impact of the Anglo-Saxons on the Anglo-Norman warrior aristocracy was seen as early as the reign of William II. New fashions—including long hair, moustaches and beards—appalled the older generation and the Church, who claimed that their youngsters looked like girls and were éffete, if not worse. In fact such fashions probably stemmed from the Anglo-Saxon styles of the previously despised 'long haired sons of the northern world'.

The old Anglo-Saxon term for a military levy, now spelt as *ferd*, remained in widespread use and was recorded in northern England as late as the end of the 13th century. The institution itself survived the conquest as a militia to be called up in case of emergency. It may even temporarily have risen in

The great hall of Hedingham Castle, Essex, as it is today; this is the largest Norman arch in Europe.

importance as many minor raids from Wales or Scotland, full-scale invasions from Scandinavia and real or threatened attacks from Normandy kept the Anglo-Norman knights fully occupied. The *ferd* was not, however, a general levy, but involved only a select group drawn from the more prosperous peasantry. The Anglo-Norman army did not consist primarily of knights, and the *ferd* even served across the Channel in Normandy, but its lack of training was a serious weakness. This was perhaps the main reason why mercenaries largely replaced the Anglo-Norman *ferd* in the 12th century.

Urban militias drawn from a 'burgess' class were closely associated with the *ferd*, and similarly consisted largely of infantry, but neither force served separately from the knights. Yet the urban militias did remain more effective, that of London being particularly famed. They not only defended their city walls but were called upon to serve in the field. Such militias could be seen as a link between the standard infantry forces of the early medieval period and the increasingly effective foot soldiers of the 14th century.

The organisation of Anglo-Norman armies reflected earlier Norman systems but was clearly more advanced. Among various senior ranks the *constable* had originally been in charge of the royal stables but now commanded the household knights. The Master Constable was in charge of court security, providing guards, door-keepers and marshals. The marshals under a master-marshal kept order, provided messengers, supervised the stables, organised hunts and had serjeants to help them. Among the full-time guards of Henry I's reign were a unit of royal archers. William II had earlier employed crossbowmen in his court, but it is not clear whether they formed a distinct unit. From such simple beginnings in an almost nomadic court a full military command structure was to evolve.

So-called household troops from the king's court were also sent to garrison important castles. Many of these were professional archers. Household knights were clearly of higher status. Many were not strictly mercenaries, as their service was reinforced by oaths of loyalty and fealty even though they received no lands in return. Such household knights also served the powerful aristocracy. Some received only pay; others held small estates while living in the lord's hall. Those holding land would not be involved in agriculture nor even in its supervision, only being concerned with the rent on which they lived.

Wealth and status varied considerably within the warrior class, but a common code of conduct was emerging and is reflected in the many epic *Chansons de Geste* which survive from the 11th and 12th centuries. This form of literature also helped to spread and strengthen the new knightly ideals which in turn reflected various influences. Above all they were a strange but powerful fusion of the previously antagonistic ideals of the Christian Church and the ancient Germanic warrior code. Honour (reputation), truthfulness, reckless courage, military skill, pride in the face of superiors and humility in the face of inferiors, protection of the weak, the Church, women and children, and a love of display were all characteristic of the *mos militum* (customs of knights). To these the *mos majorum* (customs of barons) added nobility of blood (ancestry), learning, justice and generosity.

This was, however, a strictly masculine code. A less important 'romantic' culture was growing but as yet remained separate. Women were outside the system of knightly ideals until the 12th century, when influences from the Muslim world via Spain, Sicily and the Crusades led to a mingling of the romantic and knightly ideals. The result was the unique concept of Courtly Love, which was to be central to aristocratic behaviour in the 13th and 14th centuries. In its early forms the concept of Courtly Love was more down-to-earth and closer to the ideas of the Islamic *1001 Nights* (Arabian Nights) from which it partly sprang; only later were virgin-knights and ethereal, untouched ladies to dominate the literature of Courtly Love.

On a more practical level, the ideals of warrior behaviour restrained the unbridled violence seen in

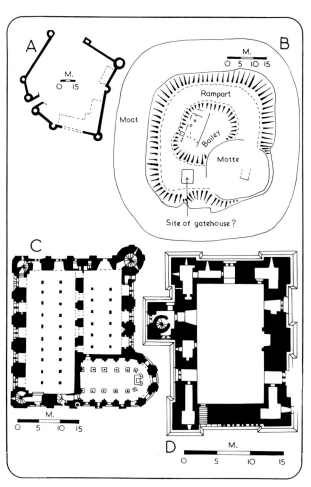

Military architecture in Normandy and England: *A* = the castle at Courcy, Calvados, built early in the 12th century during the wars between Duke Robert and Henry I of England (after Salch); *B* = the motte and bailey castle at Goltho, Lincolnshire, as it appeared *c.* 1100–50 (after Beresford); *C* = the White Tower, central keep of the Tower of London (after Tuulse); *D* = the Chambois Castle, Orne, one of the last rectangular keeps to be built in Normandy (after Tuulse).

the 10th and early 11th centuries. Even the most powerful barons generally stuck to the rules, formally renouncing fealty in an act of *diffidatio* before rebelling against their sovereign. Besieged castles were normally given an agreed time in which to ask their lord for relief. If this was not forthcoming they could surrender honourably and with minimal violence. Rarely were prisoners executed, and then only as an act of exemplary terrorism.

As equipment became more expensive so the military élite became more distinct. According to the late 11th-century *Sayings of St. Anselm*, a true knight now had to own a war-horse with bridle, saddle, spurs, hauberk, helmet, shield, sword and lance, this latter normally being of ash. The training of the Anglo-Norman knight was the same as that of his fellows in Normandy. It began when a *jeune* (youngster) of around 12 years joined a band of *amis* (comrades) to train 'like brothers' in a *compagnie* or *maisnie*. Schooling involved horsemanship, the training of horses, use of weapons, archery, self defence, wrestling, hunting, what would now be called 'fieldcraft', riding, operating as a group, and the rules of spoils and plunder. The extravagant dress of young men was part of their group solidarity, which was itself a vital element in military training. Once trained they became *armigers* (squires) but might have to wait years before being 'dubbed' as knights, often all at one time. The moment chosen for this ceremony at between 16 and 22 years of age was often unconnected with the dubbing itself. Banquets, victories or the start of campaigns were often marked by the making of knights. Given money and weapons, the new knights would then be sent to serve a lord as a group, or graduate into the household knights of the lord in whose *familia* (military household) they had trained.

Theirs was naturally a dangerous way of life. In one recorded group of 15 such *amis* three were slain in battle and one died in a fall from a horse. The lucky ones might subsequently inherit an estate, win back one lost by an ancestor, or earn a fief through their own merits. Only then would most men marry and consequently withdraw from the pool of immediately battle-ready knights. Naturally they remained warriors, but were now distracted by other responsibilities.

'Battle between English and Danes', from *Life of St. Edmund*, probably painted at Bury St. Edmunds between 1125 and 1150, and showing Anglo-Norman knights of that period; note the forward-tilted shape of the helmet skulls, and the convincing detail of the 'baggy' waists of the mail hauberks—this is the appearance of mail when belted as it has to be if the movement of the arms is to be unrestricted. (Pierpont Morgan Library, M.736 f7v, New York)

The declining ability of the landholding knights to fulfil their expected military duties was particularly noticeable in early 12th-century England. Such knights were, in fact, fast becoming the local gentry so characteristic of English rural life. When the king needed troops he often had to get them from either the household knights of his leading barons, from his own limited household or from mercenaries. Many such mercenaries were also landowners who held only small estates and therefore relied on an income as professional warriors. Some were knights, others simply soldiers. In the reigns of William the Conqueror and William II, however, the only mercenaries seem to have been poor knights serving as cavalry, but in

The west side of Dirleton Castle, built by the Scots-Norman De Vaux family in the 13th century. The upper buildings date from the 14th and 15th centuries.

Henry I's time mercenary serjeants are seen. During the civil war between Stephen and Matilda the country was reportedly flooded by mercenaries, mostly now infantry, from England, the Celtic states and the continent. Under Stephen and Henry II these mercenaries were numerous enough to form a professional army, some sections of which were grouped by ethnic origin: Bretons, Brabançons, Spaniards and men from the Welsh borders. Others were military specialists such as siege engineers, or spearmen trained to combat cavalry. As a standing army they were also available for less usual strategies such as winter campaigns.

Anglo-Norman warfare was characterised by some ambitious and large-scale strategy. New roads were cut through forests to enable an army to bypass castles and attack an enemy's heartland. A fleet could act in conjunction with an army, particularly during operations in northern Britain. The Anglo-Norman fleet seems, in fact, to have been quite an impressive force. Many ports had naval duties as 'guardians of the sea' well before the famous Cinque Ports of south-eastern England evolved. Their ships were often manned by *piratae*, a word that originally meant sailors trained to fight. Such fleets could even attempt a blockade of the English Channel against a threatened attack from Normandy. Prolonged guerrilla warfare was normally restricted to the Welsh Marches but was also seen in eastern England's marshy fen country.

The Celtic nations
The rôle that Normans played in the other nations of Britain and in Ireland is less well known. It was,

of course, also less important, yet the Norman contribution to the history of Celtic lands cannot be ignored.

Wales, for example, retained its independence throughout the Anglo-Saxon period but largely lost it to the Normans. Norman colonisation of the countryside was thin outside Pembroke in the far south-west, but most of the Welsh principalities soon became vassals of the Anglo-Norman king. In many ways the Welsh seemed to find integration into the Norman empire easier than did the Anglo-Saxons. Even as early as the reign of Henry I Welshmen owed knight service, acted as castellans and even owned castles in Norman-held territory. Southern Welshmen helped the Normans invade north Wales in 1114, and may have accompanied Henry I to France in the same year.

A rising followed the death of Henry. By then Welshmen had learned the art of cavalry warfare, modifying it to their particular needs with smaller horses and lower saddles. They almost over-whelmed the newcomers, but after the rebellion failed Norman influence grew strong, particularly in south Wales. Even traditional Welsh epic poetry was affected in the late 11th and 12th centuries, adopting English military terminology as well as the new concepts of chivalry. Welshmen continued to fight alongside Norman troops as vassals of the king, and were still deeply involved in the tangled campaigns of John's reign.

Although the Welsh aristocracy adopted some Norman styles of combat and equipment, the fighting methods of the ordinary infantry changed less. Generally speaking a long spear was the characteristic weapon of the north, and bows of the south particularly of Gwent. Whether these latter were 'longbows' or short 'flatbows' is a matter of debate. So is the question of who was influencing whom in the gradual spread of archery in war rather than merely as a hunting method. Other Welsh equipment included javelins, small shields and relatively light mail and helmets.

The Norman impact on Scotland was different but in many ways more fundamental. Normans never tried to conquer this northern kingdom, though they almost achieved a peaceful take-over. A few Normans had served King Macbeth in 1052–54, but all appear to have been slain in battle. There was, in fact, very little use of armoured

Gaelic Irish warriors on the 11th-12th century gilded container of the *Stowe Missal*. (Nat.Mus., Dublin).

cavalry in Scotland before 1100, except perhaps in the Lothians. But even so the old Celtic forms of warfare had long been under Anglo-Saxon influence. A small number of Normans did help the Anglicised King Edgar defeat a Celtic rebellion in the north and west at the end of the 11th century, and in 1114 there may have been a few Normans in the Scottish army which marched south to help Henry I. King Edgar's policy of welcoming Normans was continued by his younger brother David, who first governed southern Scotland and subsequently became king in 1124. It was he who gave large estates to his friend De Brus. This family originated from Brix in the Cotentin peninsula, and later took a leading rôle in Scottish history under the name of Bruce. The whole character of the Scottish nation had been changing since the northern kingdom of Alban conquered 'Welsh' Strathclyde and the Anglo-Saxon south-east of Scotland.

King David I, who also had large estates in central England, consciously remodelled Scotland's administration along Anglo-Norman lines. He encouraged Normans to come north by giving them senior office, thus strengthening his new feudal structure. Charters soon mention knight service,

mounted serjeants, mounted and infantry archers. Along the island-studded west coast a peculiar variation of feudalism saw land being held in return for service with longships and oarsmen. There were many such compromises between Celtic and Norman systems. In the south and centre fortified royal towns, *burghs*, sprang up to be inhabited by Englishmen, Flemings, Normans, Anglo-Danes and of course Scots. Older forms of loyalty and kindred groupings, later seen as clans, survived in the western Highlands, while in the north-east the Celtic leadership survived but transformed itself into a feudal aristocracy. In fact it was the Norman newcomers who had to earn their way into the existing power structure. Nevertheless it is worth noting that 12th-century Scottish rulers, addressing their subjects in order of importance, referred to their 'French, English, Scots, Welsh and Galwegians'. Although the Normanisation of Scotland was basically peaceful there was plenty of native resistance, both cultural and physical. Many risings were directed against the ruler and his 'foreign friends', particularly from the north and west. All

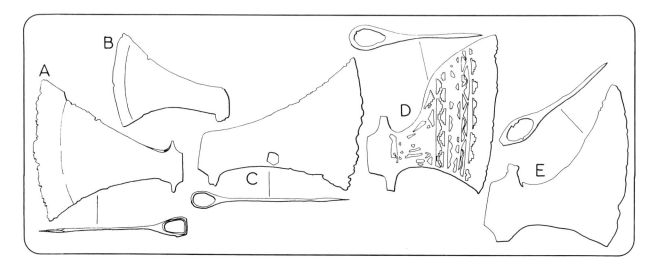

The development of the war-axe on the fringes of the Norman world: *A* = **from Caerlaverock, Anglo-Scottish border, c. 1050–1100 (Burgh Mus., Dumfries)**; *B* = **from Lumphanan, Aberdeenshire, 12th C.? (Mus. of Antiq., Edinburgh)**; *C* = **Irish, 12th C.? (Ulster Mus., Belfast)**; *D* = **probably Hebridean, from Co. Mayo, 13th C.? (Nat.Mus., Dublin)**; *E* = **Irish, from Co. Derry, 13th C.? (Nat.Mus., Dublin)**

were defeated as the building of castles spread across the land. These were of the simplest wooden motte and bailey type but, by the late 13th century, stone castles appeared. Most were built by members of a new French-speaking Scots-Norman aristocracy, such as the De Vaux family which erected Dirleton Castle in East Lothian.

Dirleton overlooks the Great North Road. This was a major feature in Border warfare, but in the 11th and 12th centuries the Anglo-Scots border was not as fixed in the minds of the two nations as it was later to become. Many Scots, not least their king, thought that the old Roman frontier of Hadrian's Wall should be their southern limit. During the troubled years following the Norman conquest of England King Malcolm of Scotland not only increased Scotland's degree of independence from English suzerainty but even pushed south, occupying the mixed Gaelic Scandinavian-speaking areas of northern Cumbria around Carlisle. This had earlier formed part of the kingdom of Strathclyde, the rest of which had been incorporated into Scotland only a generation earlier. Even the Anglo-Saxon regions of the south-east had only been taken in 1018. In 1093 the Anglo-Normans struck back, putting their client Duncan on the Scottish throne. In return the new king swore fealty to William II of England.

At the height of England's difficulties during the civil war between Stephen and Matilda the Scots took control of the rest of Cumbria and even parts of Northumberland. But within three years of coming to the throne King Henry II retook Northumbria as well as Cumbria and Carlisle. Thereafter the Border was relatively static, but raiding, official or otherwise, was endemic for centuries. It was unlike warfare in southern England or Normandy. Here speed and the winning of booty were what mattered. War had, in fact, to be self-financing, with cattle, prisoners for enslavement or ransom, equipment of all kinds and—for the Scots at least—anything made of iron being a primary objective. On the Anglo-Norman side equipment and tactics were similar to those in the south, but probably lighter and with greater reliance on archery. On the Scots side inferior equipment and a shortage of both archers and modern-style cavalry led to a reliance on large numbers of infantry spearmen supported by an élite of axe-bearers. The old Viking war axe was to see a new lease of life in Scotland, where it evolved into the Borderers' famous long-shafted Jeddart axe in the 13th and 14th centuries. In the western Highlands the axe developed slightly differently into the so-called Galloglach axe of the Hebrides and Ireland.

Ireland

The Norman impact on Ireland was different yet again. Like Scotland, Ireland was changing under English influence even before the Normans invaded the island. It was not yet feudalised but was no longer the tribal society of earlier centuries. Many

26

small Irish courts imitated the fashions of the Anglo-Norman court. Ireland was by no means culturally isolated. Trade was largely in the hands of Celto-Scandinavian *ostmen* of the Irish ports. Viking tradition was also very strong in the armament and military organisation of 11th and 12th century Ireland.

As usual, the first Normans arrived as mercenaries, probably as armoured infantry, to reinforce the light cavalry who, despite their lack of stirrups, were already the main striking power of Irish armies. Most native Irish warriors fought without armour, using short spears, javelins or broadbladed axes of Scandinavian form. Bronze maces would also appear in the 12th century. There are many descriptions of the Normans in Irish annals as 'grey foreigners' in iron mail, though the archers seem to have been more feared than the cavalry.

The invasion itself began with the recruiting of Norman and Flemish troops from south Wales by Dermot, king of Leinster. These men then called upon their own king, Henry II, for aid, and held on until he arrived in 1171. Henry's willingness to involve himself in the affair and to disguise it as a crusade was probably designed to divert Papal attention from the murder of Thomas à Becket, Archbishop of Canterbury. The Normans then went on to conquer part of eastern Ireland, but they never succeeded in subduing the whole island.

One of their main problems was a huge difference between Irish and Norman forms of warfare. This resulted in a kind of stalemate, for while the Normans fought to dominate people and land, the native Irish fought only to dominate people. The country was very under-populated and, at least in the north, the inhabitants were semi-nomadic and pastoral, their main wealth being in cattle. It was thus counterproductive to slay too many of the foe. Instead harrying, plundering and limited but highly visible destruction were designed to extort tribute and obedience. Most warfare consisted, however, of cattle raiding with minimal casualties. When the Normans tried to hold a piece of territory the inhabitants often destroyed their own homes, burned their crops and migrated to another area. The Normans retaliated by trying to force Gaelic chieftains to return such refugees and by encouraging foreigners to settle the vacated land. In response the Irish concentrated on guerrilla warfare in marsh

'Centaur' bowman wearing a conical nasal helmet: late 12th century *tympanum* showing Norman influence, *in situ* Cormac's Chapel, Cashel, Ireland.

and forest where the Normans' technological advantages were reduced to a minimum. In the 13th century Irish resistance was stiffened by the recruitment of axemen from western Scotland and the Hebrides. First recorded as *gall óglach*, foreign warriors, in 1290, these mercenaries had probably been serving in Ireland at least 50 years already.

Within the area conquered by the Anglo-Normans the whole structure of society was changing. Feudalism was imposed by force along with its associated military systems. This was at first based on military service, but a form of commutation called royal service soon became widespread as it enabled the ruler to hire and pay mercenaries. In some areas more knights' fees were created than the king had originally intended. Leinster, for example, was able to field 180 although only 100 were owed. This meant a clear profit, and increased military potential for the feudal lord. Most knights and tenants were newcomers from England or Wales. Many disbanded mercenaries from England were also encouraged to settle in new towns which were, in reality, little more than villages. Wooden fortifications were also erected in almost every new Norman manor but, except along the border between Anglo-Norman and Gaelic Ireland, these were rapidly abandoned.

Within the Anglo-Norman zone there was considerable intermarriage between the old and new military aristocracies. The Scandinavian *ostmen* also continued as a warlike burgess class in the coastal towns. Divisions between the feudalised Anglo-Norman area and the Gaelic areas beyond became sharper as the pace of Norman conquest slowed to a stop. It was along this border that most warfare naturally took place.

The areas under Anglo-Norman rule also enjoyed an economic and population boom, a huge spread of agriculture and a real social revolution which pulled Ireland into the mainstream of European history for the first time. The towns expanded, particularly the ports, as did trade. Ireland was soon exporting its light and fast horses, not only to England but to the Continent. Within two generations of the arrival of the Normans, feudal Ireland was sending its troops to fight for the Anglo-Norman king in England, Wales and France. Ulster and Kildare even saw the growth of small iron industries, though these were largely confined to the castles. The impact of such developments was also felt beyond the area of Anglo-Norman control in the Gaelic regions.

In all the Celtic nations the Norman conquests, warlike or peaceful, were incomplete. In Wales the northern principality of Gwynedd remained free

until Angevin times. In Scotland the process of Normanisation did not lead to political control by England. In Ireland the area conquered by the Anglo-Normans covered less than half the country. The reason was, of course, partly local resistance, but it also resulted from political decisions by the Norman kings themselves. Many of their potentially most troublesome and certainly most powerful barons were based in the borderlands. What better way of ensuring that they did not become 'over-mighty' than by keeping Celtic realms in being just beyond their frontiers. These small but warlike states needed little money and less prompting to descend upon their Norman neighbours should these neighbours in turn make trouble for the king.

The Normans in Italy and Sicily

The first Norman mercenaries seem to have arrived in southern Italy in 1017 to fight in a revolt against Byzantine rule. At this time the area was divided between Byzantine provinces, autonomous coastal city-states and independent Lombard principalities. Meanwhile the island of Sicily was ruled by Arab emirs owing occasional allegiance to Tunisia or Egypt. Some 12 years later the Normans began to settle around Aversa, but not until 1041 did one band of adventurers under Robert Guiscard set about conquering territory in their own right. By 1059 Norman rule over much of Apulia and Calabria was recognised by the Pope. In 1071 Bari fell, and Byzantine authority collapsed.

The invasion of Sicily had begun 11 years earlier but was not completed until 1091. The various conquered regions were at first governed separately, but were united as a single Norman state in 1127, this being recognised as a kingdom in 1130.

Almost inevitably the Normans were drawn into rivalry with the Zirid rulers of Tunisia. Early expeditions failed, but around 1134 a more determined invasion took advantage of internal Zirid squabbles, and by 1148 the Normans ruled a North African province from northern Tunisia to the Gulf of Sirte, even including the ancient Islamic city of Kairwan. This 'empire' had collapsed by

NORMAN ITALY AND SICILY c.1145 AD

Norman invasions of Byzantium
.... 1081
.... 1084-85
.... 1147
.... 1185

1160, partly because of the rising power of fundamentalist Almohades from Morocco, and partly because the heartland of the Norman state faced Byzantine invasions plus threats from the German Emperor who ruled northern Italy.

At one time it looked as if Norman ambitions against Byzantium would be more successful. These also partly grew out of commercial rivalry in the Mediterranean. Invasion and counter-invasion culminated, in 1185, in a Siculo-Norman army capturing Thessaloniki and marching to within a few days of Istanbul (Constantinople), the Byzantine capital. But they were turned back; and within a few years the Norman kingdom was itself torn apart by a disputed succession. In 1194, after years of civil war and invasion, Norman rule ended when the German Emperor Henry VI of Hohenstaufen occupied the kingdom. This, then, was the chequered history of the most cultured of the Norman states, one built firmly upon traditions which the Normans had found when they came to the area in the 11th century.

These traditions were very mixed. While Arab troops had played a secondary rôle to that of the Berbers in the previous Muslim conquest of Sicily, they took a leading role politically, culturally and in the command of most military forces. Hence their importance in the development of Siculo-Muslim forces, whose traditions were subsequently inherited by the Normans. Troops of servile or slave origin, plus mercenaries, were important but the introduction of the *iqta* (fief) and the regional *jund* (militia) systems did produce some aspects of feudalism. Both these forms of military organisation survived under the Normans. The *iqta* were transformed with little difficulty or alteration into fiefs for the new Norman Christian élite. Meanwhile the *jund* system of western Sicily, with its territorial militias based upon the *iqlim* or district, continued to provide the Normans with reliable Muslim warriors.

The many and close contacts between Muslim Sicily and southern Italy before the coming of the Normans also led to similarities in the military styles of the two regions. But whereas the population of southern Italy had been largely demilitarised under Byzantine rule, the Norman conquerors of Sicily were faced by a population of soldiers—Arabs, Berbers, local converts and others—who were prepared to defend their existing political supremacy. Later, after their defeat, the old military class of Sicily continued to fight for a new Christian king.

Italians, Byzantines and Lombards

Before looking at the Normans themselves, however, the Italians and Byzantines should be fitted into this complex military context. Both communities had an influence on the development of the Norman army, certainly on the Italian mainland and even in Sicily. The demilitarisation of the local population under Byzantine rule applied to the rural rather than urban areas. As the Byzantine *themes* of Langobardia (Apulia), Lucania and Calabria developed economically they also became administratively more self-sufficient. Around 1040 the professional *theme* armies were disbanded and responsibility for defence largely fell upon local urban militias. Such predominantly infantry forces subsequently came to terms with the Norman invaders and helped eject the Byzantine authorities. Local militias were not, of course, necessarily Greek. The population of Calabria might have been mostly so, but that of Lucania was mixed, while Langobardia, with the exception of a Greek-speaking area at the very tip of the heel of Italy, was largely Italian.

A very similar system operated in those areas under Lombard authority, where armies reflected a strong Byzantine influence. The turbulent pre-Norman duchies of Capua, Benevento and Salerno were not feudally organised and their rulers again relied primarily on urban militias. In the country-

Roseto Castle, one of the defences of the Calabrian coast of Italy. Its lower part might date from the Norman period.

Christian slaying 'pagans': early 12th century carving, *in situ* **west front, San Nicola, Bari.**

side castles were garrisoned by non-noble troops recruited by the castle's owner. In contrast there already existed in cities like Naples and Bari a class of citizens whose status and military obligations were sufficiently impressive for the Normans to enfief their cavalry élite as knights within a few years of taking control. Other cities put up such a spirited defence against the Normans—for example Capua in 1062—that the conquerors subsequently left the protection of vital gates or citadels in the hands of local citizens.

Mounted troops were also fielded by the major ecclesiastical authorities and land-owners. Nevertheless the military obligations placed upon church estates were lighter than those in Norman England. Many such church troops seem to have been mounted and armoured in the normal western European fashion. Expensive heavy cavalry equipment could probably be afforded because these church estates were generally more feudalised than were those of secular landowners. Secular militias did, however, include some armoured horsemen as well as light cavalry and numerous infantry.

These, then, were the military circumstances into which the Normans erupted so successfully in the 11th century and which they were soon to inherit. The Normans themselves were, of course, mostly armoured horsemen as they or their ancestors had been in Normandy itself. Not that Normans were the only northern Europeans to be attracted by the lure of southern Italy: Bretons, Flemings, Poitevans and men from Anjou are also recorded. But of course Normans dominated both numerically and in the leadership of the many war-bands.

In the early days their military organisation seems to have been more communal than feudal with warriors following a leader of their choice rather than a hereditary prince. The feudal military obligations that later provided the foundation of the expanding Norman state were similar to those of Normandy and England, consisting of 40 days' duty with 'hauberk and destrier' and a suitable feudal following. The number of such 'one-hauberk' knight's fees was to grow quite large—3,453 on the mainland alone, according to the *Catalogus Baronum*. This referred to the years between 1154 and 1166 but excluded Calabria and Sicily. New knight's fees that were created in Sicily tended to be small, which could indicate that they followed the pattern of the previous Muslim *iqta* land holdings. Perhaps they were also, as a consequence of their small size, large in number. Elsewhere there is mention of non-noble freeholders, probably new settlers, whose land tenure was on condition of military service. Such a structure was nevertheless firmly rooted in the pre-Norman administration. Variations between provinces also betrayed the pre-Norman foundations. In Apulia and Capua Lombard elements are visible; in Calabria, Byzantine; and in Sicily, most noticeable of all, Islamic.

The Norman rulers could not rely solely on feudal resources despite a theoretical widening of military obligations, so that the entire adult male population could be called upon to fight. The serfs or *servientes defensati* were expected to provide their own equipment, while in Sicily the villein class, whether of Lombard (Italian), Greek or Muslim origin, had to undertake specific local garrison duties. In reality, however, the growing centralisation and wealth of the Norman government seems to have led to a steady decline in reliance on local levies, particularly in traditionally well-administered areas like Calabria and Sicily. In turn there was a rapidly increasing reliance on mercenaries.

The employment of such professional soldiers introduced yet more elements into an already complex military situation. As early as 1054 Robert Guiscard recruited non-Norman Calabrians, Greeks or Slavs, for the invasion of Sicily. Troops as well as sailors were drawn from Italian states like Pisa and Genoa, these being used to garrison coastal cities as well as to man the fleet. In fact it has been suggested that the Norman rulers of Sicily relied on strictly Italian troops far more than has previously been realised. Non-Muslim as well as Siculo-Muslim troops were, of course, needed to support the feudal core of the Norman army. The Normans made war on almost all their neighbours at various times, including the rulers of North Africa. It was here that non-Muslims were required, since it seems to have been agreed that Muslim troops would not be sent against their co-religionists. Altogether the Norman field army could consist of heavy and light cavalry, some of the latter were armed with bows though probably not fighting in Turkish horse-archery fashion, plus heavily armoured and more lightly equipped infantry. Other contingents of volunteers fought without pay but for booty alone. These *rizico* seem to recall the *muttawiya* volunteers who figured so prominently in previous Muslim forces.

A Muslim landed aristocracy also survived in western Sicily. Although probably depleted and in decline, it seems to have held a number of small castles and to have fielded its own forces of both infantry and cavalry throughout the Norman period and into the early 13th century. Most of the Muslim troops serving Norman rulers were clearly mercenaries paid by the treasury rather than being a part-time militia. Though paid, their service was in a way quasi-feudal, for it was performed in return for religious toleration extended towards Islam by the Norman government. These troops formed a standing army of light cavalry, skilled siege engineers and numerous infantry, of whom the archers were renowned for their speed of movement and rate of shooting. They were organised along lines that reflected the pre-Norman territorial *jund* and were sometimes led by men of their own faith. An élite, significantly drawn from the infantry archers, also formed a guard for the Royal Treasury or *Camera*.

The impact of these archers on military

Caccamo Castle near Palermo, Sicily, built in *c.* **1160 in essentially Byzantine-Arab style. (Touring Club d'Italia)**

developments in medieval Italy might have been as strong as that of later English longbowmen on English and French tactics. Armed with powerful composite bows and short swords, they proved to be highly effective against heavy cavalry as the latter were often no more manoeuvrable than the light infantry archers. They could, in fact, sometimes move swiftly enough to act in conjunction with their own cavalry in a frontal attack. In earlier centuries the militia infantry of Italian cities had fought only with spear and shield, but in the 13th century the tactical rôle of the Normans' Siculo-Muslim light infantry archers seems to have been inherited by the famous crossbowmen of northern Italy.

The Normans of Sicily and southern Italy also inherited a flourishing, though probably small-scale arms industry. As yet it is impossible to say how the products of this industry differed from or were similar to the arms and armour of neighbouring manufacturing regions in western Europe, Byzantium, North Africa and the Middle East. Sicily was rich in iron from around Messina and Palermo, as well as in the timber needed for fuel in metal-working. Armourers had reportedly been active in late 9th-century Palermo; and Muslim Sicily had certainly shared a general economic expansion, agricultural and industrial, seen in the western provinces of Islam from the 8th to 11th centuries. A comparable, though perhaps less dramatic process of development was taking place in southern Italy from the 7th to 11th centuries. There was a growth of wealth and productivity in both the Byzantine provinces and the Lombard duchies involving agriculture, mining, metal-working and ship-building.

The lively Mediterranean trade of coastal cities like Amalfi during the pre-Norman period is well known, though the importance of Amalfi itself declined in the face of Pisan and Genoese competition from the 10th century. It is, however, worth noting that trade between the southern Italian ports of Amalfi or Salerno and the Middle East, particularly in traditional Italian cargoes like wood and iron, revived immediately after their occupation by the Normans. Thereafter it continued until relations with Egypt were ruined by Siculo-Norman attacks on the Nile Delta in 1153. In this context it should be pointed out that the Norman rulers continued their predecessors' strict state monopoly over the exploitation of forests and mines, and hence over arms production, as well as over the export of primary products.

Military equipment
Students of the arms and armour of the Norman south are fortunate because three major and almost unique sources of information survive from the early, middle and late periods. The earliest are carvings over the north door of the church of San Nicola at Bari. Dating from the very early 12th century, they are believed to illustrate an episode in the First Crusade, either the capture of Jerusalem or

Above and on p. 45 Panels from the late 12th century bronze doors of Trani Cathedral, showing St. Eustace and four Siculo-Norman warriors; note the very clear depiction of the recurved bows. (*In situ*, Trani Cathedral)

more probably the fall of Antioch. The Italo-Norman baron Bohemond of course took most of the credit for this latter victory. The five defenders of the city in this scene mostly wear a form of lamellar armour and seem to have turbans. A conical helmet, a mail hauberk and possibly two mail coifs are also shown on the defenders. One may assume that the artist modelled these figures on the closest available Muslim warriors, namely those of early Norman Sicily. The only archer in the scene is also one of these men, all of whom are on foot. Other defenders are armed with spears, swords and kite-shaped shields.

The eight horsemen who attack the city look at first sight like typical Norman knights, but closer inspection shows considerable differences. Those attacking from the left are dressed in short-sleeved mail hauberks, carry only spears and seem almost to have stepped out of the Bayeux Tapestry. Of those attacking from the right one clearly wears a mail hauberk. The other three wear lamellar or, much less likely, scale armours, one of which is put on over a mail hauberk. This group of four men are armed

Early Normandy:
1: Norman bishop, c.1050
2: Norman *miles*, c.1025
3: Flemish serjeant, c.1040

1   2   3   A

The Battle of Hastings, 14 October 1066:
1: Duke William
2: Bishop Odo
3: Breton knight
4: Norman archer
5: Infantryman from Maine
6: Anglo-Saxon *huscarl*

B

Norman England:
1: Anglo-Norman
   noblewoman, c.1140
2: Anglo-Norman squire,
   squire, c.1125–50
3: Norman knight,
   c.1100–25

D

3   1   2

The fall of Normandy:
1: Norman knight, c.1180
2: Breton serjeant, c.1160
3: Welsh auxiliary, c.1200

E

The Normans in Ireland and Scotland:
1: Anglo-Norman knight, De Clare family, c.1225
2: Gaelic Irish warrior, c.1200
3: Hebridean warrior, c.1200

F

Early Norman Italy and Sicily:
1: Siculo-Norman knight, c.1130
2: Neapolitan infantryman, c.1100
3: Sicilian infantry archer, c.1140

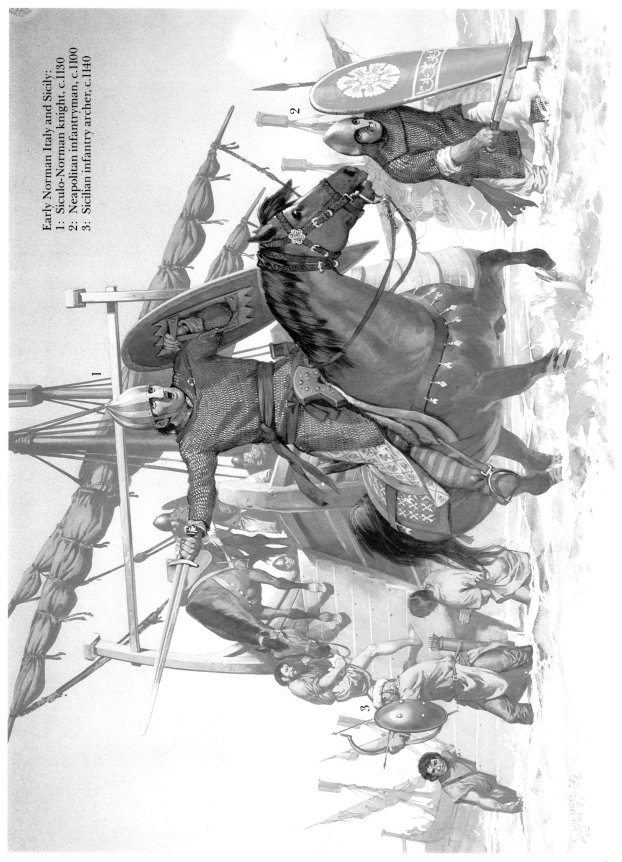

G

Later Norman Italy and Sicily:
1: Italo-Norman nobleman, c.1170
2: Siculo-Norman guardsman, c.1180
3: Sicilian levy, c.1175

H

The Normans in the East:
1: Italo-Norman Crusader, c.1098
2: Norman ex-Byzantine mercenary, c.1085
3: Oshin the Hethoumian, c.1098

I

The Principality of Antioch:
1: Knight of Antioch, c.1268
2: Norman-French Crusader, c.1250–60
3: Turcopole, c.1270

J

Castles and fortifications:
1: Mirville, 11th C.
2: Abinger, late 11th C.
3: Hedingham, 12th C.

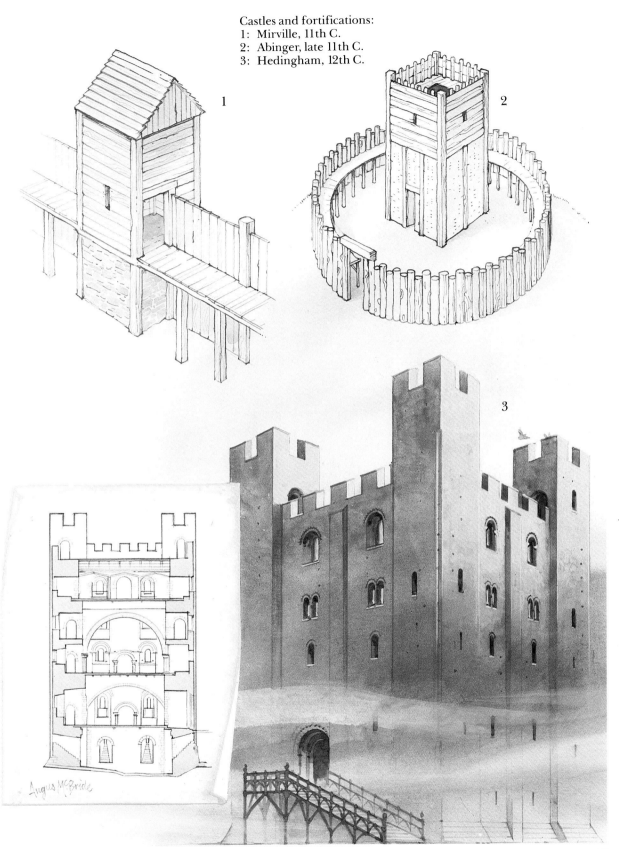

Angus McBride

K

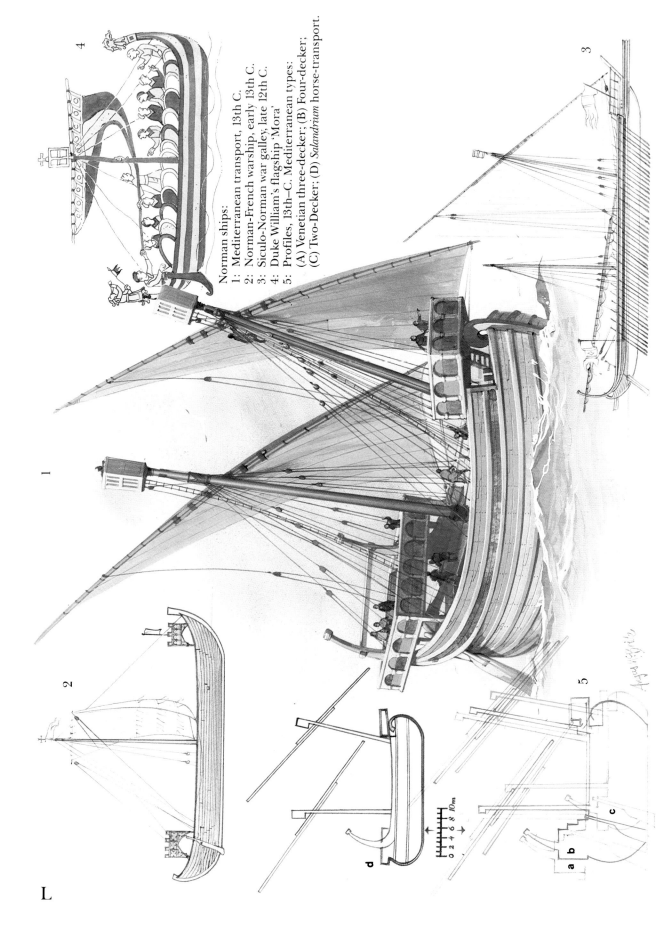

Norman ships:
1: Mediterranean transport, 13th C.
2: Norman-French warship, early 13th C.
3: Siculo-Norman war galley, late 12th C.
4: Duke William's flagship 'Mora'
5: Profiles, 13th–C. Mediterranean types:
(A) Venetian three-decker; (B) Four-decker;
(C) Two-Decker; (D) *Salandrium* horse-transport.

L

with spears or swords. Bearing in mind the already fierce antagonism between the Normans and Byzantium these lamellar-armoured horsemen are unlikely to represent Byzantine troops who, of course, played only a minor rôle in the First Crusade. Their appearance is therefore likely to indicate a high degree of lingering Byzantine influence on the arms and armour of the early, and as yet still disunited, Norman states in southern Italy.

The second major source of information is the unique Cappella Palatina ceiling in Palermo. Made of painted wooden panels in an almost purely western Islamic style in around 1140–43, it illustrates military equipment as varied as the cultures and population of Norman Sicily. It was probably made by Siculo-Muslim artists and it is natural that Islamic military styles predominate. Most, though clearly not all the warriors shown on this mid-12th-century Cappella Palatina ceiling are likely to mirror the appearance of those Siculo-Muslim warriors who served in Norman armies. Four are shown as guardsmen wearing typical Islamic ceremonial costume, and they almost certainly look like the élite units which protected the Norman ruler and his treasury. Where apparently European mail hauberks, helmets, shields and

weapons are shown, it should be borne in mind that such equipment was also used in western Islamic regions from Egypt to Spain.

The third vital source for the military equipment of Norman Sicily and, to a lesser extent, southern Italy are the carved capitals in the Cloister of Monreale Cathedral. This was built in the hills overlooking Palermo between 1174 and 1189. Although essentially late Romanesque in style, the capitals illustrate a great variety of warriors and their even more mixed equipment. They, again, probably reflect the mixed armies of later Norman Sicily, for the weaponry includes western European, Byzantine, Islamic and specifically North African styles. Four basic fashions are present. These are full mail hauberk and helmet for both cavalry and infantry; lamellar or scale armour, which is generally worn without a helmet by both cavalry and infantry; infantry wearing variously shaped helmets but no apparent body armour; and completely unarmoured cavalry and infantry. Shields are varied while weaponry is even more so, including long lance, short spear or javelin, mace,

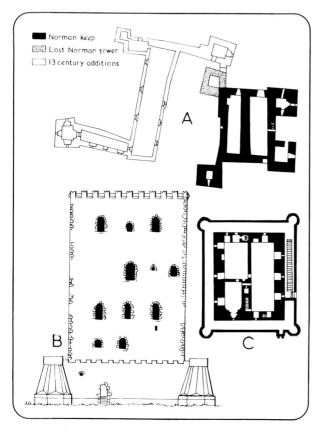

Military architecture in Norman Italy: *A* = **Melfi Castle, mid-11th C. (after Willemsen);** *B & C* = **Elevation and plan of Adrano Castle, built *c.* 1070 on ruins of an Arab tower. The lower outer wall and round towers are a later addition (after Caciagli).**

axe, short 'self-bow' of simple construction, and composite recurved bow. Swords appear as broad-bladed or pointed and almost triangular. There is even what appears to be a curved sword or sabre.

Such evidence, when added to the written sources, shows the armies of Sicily and southern Italy to have remained very varied, cosmopolitan forces up to and even beyond the fall of the Norman kingdom.

The Normans in the East

Normans are recorded in Byzantine service within a few years of their appearance in Italy. In the 11th century most of the so-called 'Franks' in Byzantium seem to have been Italo-Normans or to have arrived via southern Italy. Some came as individuals, others in groups of as many as a hundred men. Their first operations were as part of Byzantine forces fighting the Muslims of Sicily, or against Pecheneg Turkish invaders in the Balkans.

Normans rapidly rose to military prominence, a certain Hervé acting not only as leader of the Norman mercenaries in around 1050 but also as one of general Nicephorus' two chief lieutenants. Almost inevitably, these turbulent Norman leaders soon quarrelled with their paymasters; but in Byzantium, unlike Italy and so many other areas, Norman efforts to carve out their own principalities all failed. Hervé broke with Emperor Michael VI and took a force of some 300 Norman troops to eastern Anatolia. Here, however, he came up against not only the Byzantine authorities but Armenians, Seljuk Turks and finally the Arab emir Abu Nasr of Ahlat, who clapped Hervé in irons and sent him back to Byzantium. Yet Norman resilience was such that Hervé rose again to become *stratilate* of Byzantium's eastern army under Isaac Comnenus in around 1058.

There were already many Normans in Byzantine Armenia, Georgia and the Trabzon area. In 1057 two of the five eastern frontier corps consisted of 'Franks'. Their main base was Malatya. Others were based further south at Urfa (Edessa) under the command of the duke of Antioch. The next leader of these Normans was Robert Crispin, known as Crépin the Frankopoulos. He died, supposedly of Byzantine poison, shortly after the disastrous Byzantine defeat by the Seljuk Turks at Manzikert in 1071. The Normans then found a third leader in Roussel de Bailleul who had, until 1069, been one of Robert Guiscard's lieutenants in southern Italy. He then took service with Byzantium, first against pagan Turkish raiders in the Balkans and subsequently in the Emperor Romanus' catastrophic campaign of 1071.

Manzikert brought the Byzantine Empire to its knees. Seljuks, other Turks, Armenians, Kurds and Arabs now struggled to take control of various parts of Anatolia. Roussel saw the potential of such a situation, and set out to create a Norman principality in the east. He came closer to success than had his predecessors, yet he too failed. From the fief that the Byzantines had given him in Armenia he fought against all comers but, like Hervé before him, Roussel was captured by the

Muslims and sent back to his one-time foe, the future Emperor Alexius I Comnenus. Four years later Roussel also re-emerged into imperial favour as the leader of the 'Frankish' mercenaries of Alexius I.

The fate of many other Normans in eastern Anatolia is more obscure and perhaps even stranger. This strategic area had been strongly garrisoned by the Byzantines, who generally sent their best western mercenaries there. After the disaster of Manzikert many of these Normans or 'Franks' helped the Turks destroy the Byzantines' Armenian vassal states of Taron and Sassoun. But a revival of Armenian independence then occurred further south in the Taurus mountains, Cilicia and northern Syria. Some 8,000 'Franks' under a certain Oursel also moved down to the upper Euphrates Valley and the northern edge of the Syrian plain. Here many cities continued to recognise nominal Byzantine authority while paying tribute to the victorious Muslims. They survived, in fact, as pawns in the greater struggle between Seljuk Turks and the Arab emirs of Syria, but their autonomy was real enough. An Armenian general called Philaretus seized control of one such city, Antioch, in 1079. Originally Philaretus had commanded Byzantine forces along the south-eastern frontier, and as such he was well known to the Normans. Philaretus then went on to take control of a broad territory which included Urfa

Sperlinga Castle near Enna, Sicily, was built on and partly inside a mountain. Little is known of its early history, but it probably includes elements from all periods: Byzantine, Islamic, Norman and later. (Touring Club d'Italia).

(Edessa). He is also said to have commanded an army of up to 20,000 warriors, the most effective element of which were the supposedly 8,000 Normans or 'Franks' who, under their new leader Raimbaud, had joined Philaretus as early as 1073.

Their first base was a fortress called Afranji, the 'Franks'' castle, near Harput on the left bank of the Euphrates. Others joined the garrison of Urfa and perhaps Antioch. Raimbaud himself died while defending Philaretus' tent against Thornig, the Armenian prince of Sassoun in 1074. It may also be no coincidence that merchants from Amalfi in Norman-ruled southern Italy continued to trade with Antioch during these troubled years, or that men from Bari, one of the main cities of Norman Italy, were trading at Tarsus in Cilician Armenia as late as 1097.

The career of Philaretus and perhaps of his Norman supporters came to an abrupt end around 1085, when the Seljuk Turks first captured Antioch then went on to crush both the Arab dynasties ruling Mosul and Aleppo and their Armenian ally Philaretus. Urfa itself fell in 1087 by treachery from within the walls. The city did, however, retain its autonomy under Armenian governors. Urfa also kept its own forces to defend the city and garrison outlying castles. These were primarily an urban militia, though mercenaries were hired when money was available. The fate of the Normans after this Seljuk take-over is unrecorded, but according to Crusader sources the warriors of Urfa at the time that the First Crusade arrived were armed and armoured in what sounds like European style. Elsewhere, particularly in Antioch, the old military class of Armenians and Greeks were 'Turcified'— *turcaverant*—through intermarriage with the conquering Seljuks. A substantial section of the previous élite clearly came to terms with the newcomers, and it was they, or their descendants, who reportedly fled at the approach of the Crusaders. 'Franks' or Normans are not specifically mentioned. Nevertheless only 12 years separated the Seljuk seizure of Antioch and the arrival of the First Crusade. Might the offspring of Norman mercenaries, legitimate or otherwise, have been defending the city when Norman knights from southern Italy drew up beneath Antioch's walls?

Following the disaster at Manzikert Byzantium lost its main Anatolian recruiting grounds and so,

under the Comnenid dynasty, Byzantine forces were increasingly dominated by mercenaries, amongst whom Normans continued to form an important element. A polyglot army was recruited from these Normans plus Germans, Frenchmen and troops from the Crusader states, particularly from the Norman principality of Antioch, which was at various times a theoretical vassal of the Byzantine Empire. The main Byzantine armies were, in fact, remodelled along essentially Norman-French feudal lines by the Emperor Manuel Comnenus, great emphasis being placed on heavy cavalry using the couched lance. This process led to further disaster at Myriokephalon in 1176, where the Byzantine Empire suffered a catastrophic defeat at the hands of the Seljuks second only to that suffered at Manzikert a century earlier. Crusaders from Antioch formed Manuel's right wing at Myriokephalon. After the defeat the Emperor also sent a letter to Henry II of England, praising the courage

of Manuel's Englishmen—almost certainly referring to Anglo-Saxon troops in his service.

Many Normans also fought for Byzantium against their fellow countrymen under Robert Guiscard of southern Italy. Others were recruited to fight Pechenegs and Seljuks in the 1080s and 1090s. 'Franks' were found in the garrison defending Iznik (Nicea) in 1113, Corfu in 1149 and Varna in 1193. Others were involved in the civil war of 1180, while 'Franks' served Theodore Lascaris, ruler of Iznik, in 1259.

Many such mercenaries settled in Byzantium and founded long-lasting military families. These would often have held *pronoia*, the Byzantine equivalent of the western fief. The feudalisation of Byzantium may, in fact, have been a legacy of the days when the Comnenid Emperors recruited as many

Normans and other westerners as they could find. Among those families founded by 'Franks' were the Raoulii, who were descended from a certain Italo-Norman named Raoul, and the Petraliphae, descended from Pierre d'Aulps. A group of warrior families called the Maniakates, descended from Normans serving the great Byzantine general Maniakes, settled in Albania. Here they were led by a certain Constantine Humbertopoulos, whose name indicated descent from a westerner called Humbert. In 1201 a Constantine Frangopoulos ('son of the Frank') was given command of six war-galleys; and in 1285 another Humbertopoulos

Ivory chessmen from southern Italy or Sicily, probably 11th century; note clear details of equipment, which is almost entirely in Byzantine or western Islamic style. (Cabinet des Medailles, Bib.Nat., Paris)

defended Mesembria in present-day Bulgaria against the Mongols.

From around 1190 to 1216 the first medieval Albanian state won a brief independence under native *archons*. It would be interesting to know if any of these claimed 'Frankish' or Norman descent. Certainly when the Angevins of southern Italy created a puppet Albanian state in 1272 many local lords readily adopted feudal titles and associated forms of behaviour.

In the First Crusade Normans played a disproportionately large rôle. They were also doubly represented, with Normans from Normandy forming one contingent and Normans from southern Italy forming a second, perhaps even more important force. This was led by Bohemond of Taranto, a disinherited son of Robert Guiscard. The Italo-Normans might have been few in number but they were well equipped, well led, and disciplined—and above all, they had experience of dealing with Byzantines and Muslims.

The Principality of Antioch

This book is not about the Crusades as such (see MAA 75 *Armies of the Crusades*), but the conquest of Antioch during the First Crusade and the subsequent establishment of the principality of Antioch did create yet another Norman state. Whereas Duke Robert of Normandy and the bulk of his troops left the Holy Land in 1099, a large part of the Italo-Norman contingent remained. Bohemond was already in effective control of Antioch, but the Normans' right to rule this city did not go

unchallenged. Byzantium claimed at least suzerainty over the ancient 'duchy of Antioch', while many non-Norman Crusaders felt that Bohemond had been more interested in winning a fief than in conquering Jerusalem for the Cross. Then, in 1100, Bohemond was captured by the Danishmandid Turks, and his nephew Tancred was summoned north from Galilee to take command. While in Palestine Tancred had learned to win the active help of local Christian communities. In Antioch he used this experience to enlarge and consolidate the new principality. Tancred also encouraged Normans from Italy, Sicily and France to settle in northern Syria. He structured the new state along strictly Norman and strongly feudal lines, making it different from the kingdom of Jerusalem which was emerging to the south. At the same time Tancred recruited assorted mercenaries and found allies even among local Turkish chieftains.

Despite these efforts and those of his successors, the essentially western principality of Antioch was never able fully to establish itself in the mosaic of Middle Eastern states. Nor were its Norman military élite able to integrate themselves into Syrian society. They remained a thinly spread aristocracy which stayed alien despite sometimes adopting local, and particularly Armenian customs. The Normans and other westerners were isolated from the Muslims of the countryside by their religion and by the obligation to combat Islam with the sword. They were also separated from the local, largely urban Christians. These, though divided amongst themselves, far outnumbered the Normans, and were in turn regarded as heretics or schismatics. The only local community with whom the Normans built up a close working relationship were the Armenians, who were also a warrior people with their own neighbouring independent and to some extent feudally-organised states. Efforts to go beyond mere collaboration to political and religious union came to nothing: the cultural gulf was too wide. On an everyday military level Norman-Armenian co-operation, which had begun even before the conquest of Antioch, seems to have been commonplace. It was probably a man of

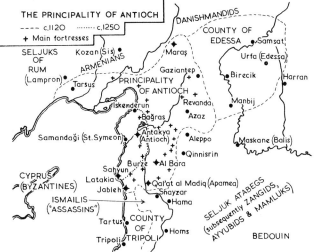

Right
Ivory cover of *Queen Melisende's Psalter* from early 12th century Crusader states, showing armour in European, Byzantine and Islamic styles. (Brit.Mus., London)

Bagras Castle overlooks the Orontes River and the Syrian plains beyond. Much of the walls date from the Armenian period, but it was a key position in the defence of Antioch.

harness, spurs, maces, some form of armour, sword scabbards and wood-framed saddles.

The direct line of Norman princes of Antioch ended as early as 1130 with the death of Bohemond II. Subsequent rulers were descended from his daughter Constance and a French nobleman, Raymond of Poitiers, who had been summoned secretly from the Norman court of Henry I of England. Feelings of *Normanitas* nevertheless remained strong in Antioch, and no less than five more princes were named Bohemond, including the last.

The feudal structures that the first Norman princes built along Siculo-Norman lines also remained relatively unchanged to the end. Feudal ties were simpler than in Europe, because the military élite was tiny and fewer people were involved. Compared with the situation in Tripoli and Jerusalem the ruler of Antioch kept most of the land and castles in his own hands during the 12th century. Almost all the big fiefs were held by his relatives, the others generally being held by men of Norman origin. The great offices of state were typically Norman, with *constables, marshals, seneschals, chamberlains, vicomtes, bailiffs* and *chatelains*. The only Byzantine or Islamic offices tended to be legal or administrative, and even these are likely to reflect Norman experience in Sicily and southern Italy. In the cities, however, administration reflected a mixture of Byzantine, Islamic and newer Italo-French ideas, while in the countryside Arab-Islamic systems continued to operate.

The organisation of Antioch's armies was overwhelmingly Western. Cavalry were, of course, the most important element. All the Crusader states suffered from a severe shortage of horses during the early years, but the principality's problems were less acute, as the plains of northern Syria had long been famous as a horse-rearing region.

The small size of Crusader armies has often been exaggerated, as has the larger numbers of their Muslim foes; yet the total of Antiochene knights never rose much above 500. In the Middle East, however, the military obligations of such knights appear to have been open-ended and were not limited to the theoretical 40 days seen in Europe. Such numbers could be considerably increased by pilgrims and landless mercenaries, from Europe. Antioch's wealth enabled it to pay for many

Armenian origin, an armourer or his descendant, who betrayed Antioch to the Crusaders in the first place. An Armenian engineer from Antioch designed siege machines which the Crusaders used against Tyre in 1124. Armenian troops served in the garrisons of Antioch and Margat in 1118. At other times as many as 4,000–5,000 Armenian horsemen and 10,000 infantry were said to be employed by the Crusader states.

The principality of Antioch and the associated county of Edessa were in some respects separate from the other Crusader states of Tripoli and Jerusalem. Their political, economic and even defence considerations were often different. Antioch's position on the ancient trade route from Iraq and Iran to the Mediterranean also made it the richest of the Crusader states. Antioch itself was a flourishing centre of commerce and industry, famous for its textiles and glass. Many westerners came to settle in the cities, and such immigrants may eventually have formed half the urban population. Though neither knights nor professional warriors, they were probably the basis of the state's infantry levy. But despite this flourishing commerce and wealth, the importance of Antioch actually declined under Crusader rule, Muslim Aleppo gradually taking over as the commercial centre of northern Syria.

Iron was mined in the mountains and the associated iron-working tradition included a small arms industry. Most of the iron-working was done around Marash, but the area as a whole had, as recently as the 10th century, produced horse-

Revanda (Ravendel) Castle was a typical outlying fortress of the Principality of Antioch. It was built on a mountain near the eastern frontier.

mercenaries who remained vital to the expansion and survival of all Crusader states. There were also many serjeants of inferior status but similar military effectiveness, plus Turcopoles, and large numbers of allies including Armenians. One large castle could have a garrison of almost 1,700 in time of peace, though only 50 of these would have been knights. In time of war the garrison could rise to 2,200.

Tactics remained basically the same as those used by the Normans in Europe, but modifications based upon local experience did soon develop. In open country the cavalry were normally preceded or even boxed in by infantry armed with spears, bows or crossbows. Such infantry defended themselves with tall shields, spearmen being in front and their ranks opening to let horsemen make their charges. In the early 12th century all the cavalry operated together, knights and non-noble warriors, fully and more lightly equipped men. Faster and more mobile forces in which infantry were mounted were also used to intercept convoys and to raid deep inside enemy territory. Light cavalry, with spears of bamboo and perhaps javelins, appeared at the end of the 12th century, modelled on Arab rather than on the more specialised and alien Turkish horse-archer traditions. By this time the Crusader states had stopped expanding and had already been forced onto the defensive, thus perhaps becoming more ready to learn. In the 13th century tactics became more flexible, varied and sophisticated.

Infantry had grown in importance, as archers and crossbowmen proved to be the best defence against horse-archers. Earlier tactics were still used, but at other times the cavalry formed up in groups outside an infantry formation into which they could retreat if necessary. They now often made more limited tactical charges by one or two smaller groups of horsemen. Mounted serjeants still fought alongside the knights but were generally less heavily armoured.

Most Turcopoles appear to have been cavalry although they also included infantrymen. Their exact origins and even their function are still a matter of debate. A number of local Christians seem to have been enrolled as serjeants but they remained few. Many more Muslim prisoners of war had been converted to Christianity in the early 12th century, and may then have fought for their new masters. Such men are unlikely to have risked returning to the Muslim fold, as apostasy from Islam was a capital offence. Turcopoles were, in fact, almost invariably executed if captured. The few recorded names of Turcopoles also suggest Muslim family origins. The evidence indicates that although many fought as horse-archers this was not in Turcoman nomadic style. Instead Turcopoles seem to have been equipped more like the *ghulams* of the neighbouring Muslim states[1]. These fought both as light cavalry and as disciplined horse-archers who shot in ranks, often at rest rather than on the move as did the tribal Turcomans. Some Turcopoles even held fiefs, which were normally listed as *serjeantries*.

The most enduring monuments of the principality of Antioch are its castles. Some were immense, and they still crown many of the hills of north-western Syria and southern Turkey. Most, however, were built during the principality's period of decline. The only big castle to be built in the 12th century was that at Sahyun; no less than 170,000 tons of virgin rock were cut away to make its eastern ditch. Smaller fortifications were also erected at this time, many overlooking mountain passes between the coast and the Muslim regions of inland Syria. Such castles were often updated structures from the 9th or 10th centuries, having originally defended the Byzantine duchy of Antioch or the Arab province of Aleppo. Most of the other cities and towns had been fortified by Byzantines, Armenians or Arabs before the Normans arrived.

During the 13th century important castles were sold to the Templers, Hospitallers or other military orders because the rulers of Antioch were increasingly short of cash and men to garrison these defences. Massive and sophisticated as they were, the castles ultimately failed, the main reason again being shortage of manpower. Antioch itself fell after a five-day siege in 1268 because the garrison could not man all its towers. Many castles were betrayed from the inside, and this tendency might have been a particularly serious example of the defensive, almost defeatist 'castle mentality' which gripped the Crusader states in the 13th century.

The military élite can hardly be blamed for such an attitude. From the time of Saladin their position became ever more obviously untenable. The county of Edessa had long gone and Antioch, like Tripoli and Jerusalem, controlled a shrinking area of countryside. Fiefs became fewer, until almost the whole knightly class was town-based. They still claimed feudal rights over villages and fields long retaken by Islam, but their status was maintained as a legal fiction unsupported even by wealth. The European settlers fled to the towns or back to Europe while a substantial number, including serjeants and maybe even knights, adopted Islam and became renegades. In 1223 the Patriarch of Alexandria claimed, perhaps with exaggeration, that about 10,000 such renegades were in Ayyubid service in Egypt and Syria. After the Fourth Crusade captured Istanbul (Constantinople) in 1204 large numbers of knights, serjeants and Turcopoles left Syria to seek their fortunes in Greece.

Military architecture in the Principality of Antioch: *A* = a stretch of the southern wall of Antioch in its original condition, as repaired in the 10th century; *B* = the castle of Sahyun (after Muller-Wiener).

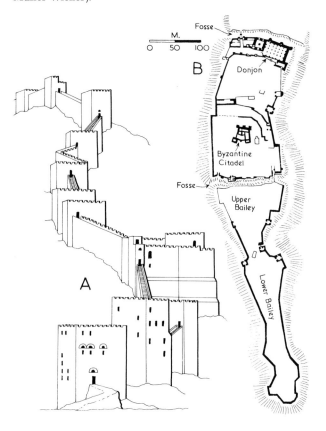

[1]Cf. MAA 171, *Saladin and the Saracens*.

Nevertheless, the principality of Antioch clung on for another 83 years. It survived in name after Antioch itself fell to the Mamluk Sultan Baybars in an orgy of slaughter and destruction. Thereafter the principality consisted of little more than the port of Lattakieh, which itself fell in 1287 after an earthquake seriously damaged its walls. Ironically, the Mamluk Sultan Qalaun justified its seizure during a time of truce by using a legal nicety that the Normans themselves might have appreciated. As the current ruler of Antioch, Qalaun claimed that he had a right to all the old principality including Lattakieh, the remaining unconquered portion. Its last prince, Bohemond VII, died childless and perhaps broken-hearted six months later.

Further reading

A great deal has been written about Norman history. Listed below are a selection of the most important journals, books and authors who have specialised in the subject:

Anglo-Norman Studies (originally *Proceedings of the Battle Conference in Anglo-Norman Studies*); first published in 1978, this journal is essential reading for any student of Norman military history.
Boüard, Michel de; for the Normans in Normandy.
Brown, R. Allen; for the Normans in England and Normandy.
Cahen, C., *La Syrie du Nord a l'époque des Croisades* (Paris, 1940)
Douglas, D. C.; for the Normans in general.
Haskins, C. H.; for the Normans in general.
Jamison, E.; for the Normans in Italy.
Le Patourel, *The Norman Empire* (Oxford, 1976)
Ménager, L. R.; for the Normans in Italy.
Musset, L.; for the Normans in Normandy.
Norwich, J. J.; for the Normans in Italy.
Yewdale, R. B., *Bohemond I, Prince of Antioch* (Princeton, 1924)

'David and Goliath', from a late 11th-century Norman manuscript. (*St. Augustine's Commentaries*, Ms.A.19, Bib.Munic., Rouen)

The Plates

A: Early Normandy:
A1: Norman bishop, c. 1050
A close alliance between Church and state was one of the great strengths of Normandy. The Church's power lay in the hold it had over an uneducated but pious military élite, a hold strengthened by the Church's virtual monopoly of art and ceremonial splendour. The bishop's 'uniform' was rigidly defined. Here he wears an early form of mitre and a T-shaped strip of embroidered cloth, the pallium, around his shoulders. Beneath his fine woollen cloak or chasuble the two gilded fabric tassels of his stole can be seen. These went over a lighter dalmatic which was in turn worn over a white linen alb. His ivory-headed crozier was a symbolic 'weapon' in God's good fight. (Sources: Bede's Commentaries, mid-12th cent. St. John's Coll., Ms.H.6, Cambridge; and various surviving vestments.)

A2: Norman miles, *c. 1025*
The early Norman *miles* or knight was equipped in identical fashion to other northern French cavalry-

men. If anything he seems to have been rather old-fashioned, and this man illustrates this trend. His mail hauberk is slit at the sides, a style originally designed for foot combat, and his shield is of the old round type. He is armed with a fine new sword but also carries javelins as well as a heavier lance. (Sources: Bible, early 11th cent. Bib.Munic., Arras; *Reliquary of St. Hadelin*, 1046, St. Martin's Church, Visé.)

A3: Flemish serjeant, c. 1040

Mercenaries from the west of Belgium became much in demand during the 11th century. This man is armed with an early form of crossbow entirely of wood. Its release mechanism consisted of a peg which simply pushed the string out of a notch when the trigger was raised. Such weapons survived in Scandinavia for many centuries. (Sources: *Commentaries of Hayman of Auxerre*, c. 1000, Bib.Nat., Ms.Lat. 12302, Paris; crossbow from Lillöhus, 15th–16th cents., Kristianstads Mus.)

B/C: The Battle of Hastings, 14 October 1066:

This scene is based primarily on the Bayeux Tapestry. The famous tapestry is, however, not only difficult to interpret but was also made some years after the event. Other pictorial sources must, therefore, be used to back up the Bayeux Tapestry.

B/C1: Duke William of Normandy

The Norman leader wears the most advanced armour of his day. It includes a one-piece iron helmet with a broad, decorated nasal. A major controversy in the Bayeux Tapestry concerns rectangular patches shown on the chests of some Normans. They are not seen on men engaged in combat, and their nearest parallels in 11th-century Spanish and French art clearly indicate unlaced mail *ventails*. The same is almost certainly true of the cruder Bayeux Tapestry. The shape of such Norman throat- and chin-covering *ventails* is, however, unknown. They might have consisted of lined or unlined mail flaps laced on both sides of the head, as shown here; or they could indicate ordinary *ventails* laced on one side of the head, inaccurately rendered by English seamstresses. The duke also wears additional mail sleeves similar to the mail *chausses* that protect his legs. The Bayeux Tapestry portrays warriors in what look like mail hauberks with trouser-like legs. Such unlikely armours are unknown anywhere else, so what might be indicated is the tying of the hems of a divided hauberk around the knees. The wooden club or *baculus* held by Duke William was not a real weapon but was probably a symbol of authority with semi-magical pagan origins. We depict the incident during the battle when William rode among his men with helmet raised to quell a panicky rumour that he had been killed.

B/C2: Bishop Odo

On the Bayeux Tapestry the duke's brother Bishop Odo is shown in a form of armour quite distinct from that of other figures. It is sometimes identified as a scale hauberk, or as a different convention for indicating mail, but the garment could also be seen as an early example of the *jazerant*, a mail-lined and padded coat of Middle Eastern origin. The bishop uses a mace of the flanged variety, which also had Mediterranean origins; and his helmet might also show Byzantine influence with its decorative finial and a medallion or reliquary at the front.

B/C3: Breton knight

This man has the equipment of an average northern French horseman consisting of a hauberk and helmet, here shown with its segments painted. The laces hanging from his neck might be to tighten the lining of his helmet and the mail coif. Some hauberks on the Tapestry seem to have scabbards passing through them twice.

B/C4: Norman archer

Some of the Norman archers on the Tapestry appear to be well-equipped professionals. Others may be a peasant levy or, more likely, sailors from the Norman fleet who had followed the army into battle. This man uses a simple selfbow—not of the massive proportions seen among 14th-century English archers, but an earlier hunting weapon which could also be used in war at sea.

B/C5: Infantryman from Maine

Professional infantry played an important part in Duke William's army, but they do not seem to be shown on the Bayeux Tapestry. This man is based on other sources and represents a warrior from the southern parts of the Norman realm. His round

helmet of two-piece construction is of a form that probably survived in France from late Roman times. His oval shield appears in a number of places, including carvings from Normandy itself. (Sources: carved capitals, late 11th cent., churches at St. Nectaire and Rucqueville.)

B/C6: Anglo-Saxon huscarl

Harold Godwinson's bodyguard of *huscarls* were the best equipped troops in the Anglo-Saxon army, and their descendants were soon employed by the Norman kings. Their arms and armour differed only in detail from those of their Norman foes. Some appear to have had separate mail coifs, though this is debatable; and they relied primarily on the long-hafted Danish axe. Many used kite-shaped shields, but some still carried round or slightly oval versions.

D: Norman England:

D1: Anglo-Norman noblewoman, c. 1140

The aristocratic fashions of 12th-century ladies were simple yet flattering. Gowns seem to have been cut on the cross which made them hug the figure. Young women also wore their hair in an extravagantly long plait, often with false hair added for extra length. Wealth was demonstrated by abundantly wide sleeves revealing a closely pleated undergarment of linen.

D2: Anglo-Norman squire, c. 1125–50

The rise of courtly culture was accompanied by an elaboration of male costume, though as yet by few changes in military equipment. Helmets had a foreward tilt which probably indicated that the front was much thicker than the sides and back. Some were clearly painted in semi-heraldic patterns, which were also appearing on shields. The young squire shown here has been serenading his lady on a psaltery—apparently with some success . . . (Sources: gilt bronze pyx, early 12th cent., Glasgow Museums and Art Galleries.)

D3: Norman knight, c. 1100–25

A number of small but important developments did take place in arms and armour around the year

1100. Hauberks became slightly longer, and usually had full-length sleeves. Shields kept the same shape but had grown to enormous proportions. This man's helmet is of an unusual fluted form with a chin-strap attached directly to the rim. The function of his headcloth is unclear, but might be a fashion adopted by some men who had returned from Crusade in Syria or Palestine. (Sources: *Bury Bible*, 1121–48, Corpus Christi Coll., Ms.2, Cambridge; carved capitals, *c.* 1120, Cathedral, Vezelay.)

E: The Fall of Normandy:
E1: Norman knight, c. 1180
The main change in arms and armour during the 12th century was the appearance of mailed mittens on the hauberk. A few helmets were also given face-masks, and from this the 'great helm' (so-called barrel helm) was later to develop. The helmet shown here is not segmented but consists of a one-piece dome reinforced with external iron strips. His shield is similarly strengthened with decorative iron straps. Under his hauberk the knight also wears a padded aketon or gambeson. (Sources: lost tomb of Count William of Flanders, mid-12th cent., St.

'St. Benedict frees a prisoner', a manuscript illustration of *c.* 1070 from Monte Cassino. (Ms.Lat. 1202, Vatican Lib., Rome)

Omer; *Legend of Roland*, stained glass window, *c.* 1218, Cathedral, Chartres; wall paintings, late 12th early 13th cents., Church of All Saints, Claverly.)

E2: Breton serjeant, c. 1160
Few differences were yet apparent in the equipment of knights and serjeants, except that the latter was more basic. The conical helmet was fast falling out of fashion, to be replaced by a rounded form. Specialised types of infantry shield also seem to have been used, the large example shown here almost being a mantlet. This serjeant wears the old arms of the Marshal of England. (Sources: painted marriage chest, 1150–70, Cathedral Treasury, Vannes; *Bible*, 1160–70, Cathedral Library, Winchester.)

E3: Welsh auxiliary, c. 1200
Little is known about 12th- and 13th-century Welsh military equipment, so this man has been given some of the more unusual items possibly used by light infantry from a Celtic area. Various types of flat-topped helmet were seen even before the appearance of the flat-topped 'great helm'. Some were associated with areas under Scandinavian influence. The war-hammer may primarily have been for trial by combat and is often associated with a relatively light egg-shaped shield. (Sources: *Guthlac Roll*, *c.* 1200, Brit.Lib., Harl.Roll Y.6; *Lewis Chessmen*, 1150–75, Brit.Mus.; effigy, *c.* 1225, Malvern Abbey; manuscript, late 12th cent., Bib.Munic., Ms. 12, St. Omer.)

F: The Normans in Ireland and Scotland:
F1: Anglo-Irish knight of the De Clare family, c. 1225
The Norman-Irish aristocracy were naturally equipped in the same style as their relatives in England. Only later did they adopt the light cavalry styles of Gaelic Ireland. This man has an early form of 'great helm' which would be worn over a padded arming cap to support its square top. The high shoulders of his surcoat indicate a thickly padded gambeson or even a semi-rigid leather 'cuirie' worn beneath. This man also has padded cuisses over his thighs and knees. (Sources: lost early 13th cent. effigies in the Temple Church, London; statues, 1230–40, west front of Cathedral, Wells.)

F2: Gaelic Irish warrior, c. 1200

Anglo-Norman styles spread only slowly into 'native' or Gaelic Ireland. This man's helmet clearly shows outside influence but his reliance on a small leather buckler and javelins is more traditional. (Sources: *Cumdach of the Stowe Missal*, 11th–12th cents., Royal Irish Academy; *Chapter House Liber A*, Public Records Office, London; carved relief, 12th–13th cents., Cashel.)

F3: Hebridean warrior, c. 1200

Scots mercenaries took part in Irish wars from an early date. In the 13th century their armoured axemen were recruited to counter armoured Anglo-Irish cavalry and infantry. This man wields a typical silver-inlaid Scots-Irish axe but his sword, with its bronze hilt, indicates a continuing link with Scandinavia. (Sources: *Lewis Chessmen*, 1150–75, Brit.Mus.; axes, 13th cent., Nat.Mus., Dublin.)

G: Early Norman Italy and Sicily:
G1: Siculo-Norman knight, c. 1130

Although the Normans continued to use the tactics of northern France after settling in Italy, their equipment soon reflected southern influences, which generally meant that slightly less armour was worn. Here the knight has no coif, relying solely on a tall conical helmet and a mail hauberk, sword and shield. Such warriors would have been virtually indistinguishable from their Italian, Byzantine and Egyptian neighbours. (Sources: painted ceiling, c. 1140, Cappella Palatina, Palermo; carved reliefs, early 12th cent., Cathedral, Lucca.)

G2: Neapolitan infantryman, c. 1100

A number of pictorial sources show southern Italian warriors using arms and armour very different from that seen in the north, and almost certainly reflecting Byzantine or Islamic influence. This man wears a helmet with a mail aventail fastened to its rim. Such a system was normal in the Middle East and Central Asia, but would not be seen in most of western Europe until the 14th century. His flat-based shield is typical of Italian infantry, while his peculiar sword is an early form of falchion. (Sources: ivory chessmen, late 11th cent., Bib.Nat., Paris; ivory alterback, 12th cent., Cathedral Mus., Salerno; carved relief from Porta Romana, mid-12th cent., Sforza Castle Mus., Milan.)

G3: Sicilian infantry archer, c. 1140

The Muslim archers of Sicily were among the most effective infantry in 12th-century Europe. Most were unarmoured, but this man has been given a light mail hauberk which he wears over a perhaps padded cap. His powerful composite bow is of an early form used throughout the Middle East and Mediterranean before the spread of Turkish influence. The system of shooting 'under' his leather shield was a technique still being used by the 14th-century Mamluks. (Sources: painted ceiling, c. 1140, Cappella Palatina, Palermo; carved relief, c. 1140, La Martorana, Palermo.)

H: Later Norman Italy and Sicily:
H1: Italo-Norman nobleman, c. 1170

By the late 12th century the arms and armour of Norman Italy seem to have drawn closer to those of the rest of the country. This splendidly equipped nobleman has a partially gilded helmet with a face-mask, worn over a separate mail coif covered in rich material. The rest of his equipment is straightforward except that the feet of his mail chausses appear to be covered in iron scales, a remarkably advanced idea for the period. (Sources: carved capitals, late 12th cent., Cathedral Cloisters, Monreale; *Murder of Becket*, wall painting, late 12th cent., Church of Sts. John and Paul, Spoleto.)

H2: Siculo-Norman guardsman, c. 1180

This man has been given a number of pieces of equipment that made their appearance in Italy towards the end of the 12th century, some of which might have been of Byzantine or Balkan inspiration. They include a kind of early salet with the brim extended to protect the back of the neck, and a broad, almost triangular short-sword. His crossbow is of a Middle Eastern composite form in which the stock appears to have a footstep jutting from the back: this might have served the same function as a loading stirrup. (Sources: carving, late 12th cent., Cathedral, Modena; wall paintings, late 12th–early 13th cents., Basilica crypt, Aquileia; military treatise by Al Tarsusi, late 12th cent., Bod.Lib., Ms. Hunt 264, Oxford.)

H3: Sicilian levy, c. 1175

The Muslim inhabitants of western Sicily were called up in times of emergency, when they had to provide their own rudimentary equipment. This man is fortunate to possess a helmet and a scale cuirass of perhaps Near Eastern or Byzantine origin. His chief weapon is a staff-sling, which would have been used in siege-warfare. (Sources: carved capitals, late 12th cent., Cathedral Cloisters, Monreale; *Chronicle of Peter of Eboli*, late 12th–early 13th cent., Bürgerbib., Berne.)

I: The Normans in the East:
I1: Italo-Norman Crusader, c. 1098
Here a warrior, a serjeant judging by his lack of spurs, delivers a message from Tancred to the Armenian lord, Oshin of Lampron. The serjeant's lamellar cuirass betrays the high degree of Byzantine influence lingering in parts of Norman Italy, particularly in Apulia. (Sources: carved relief, very early 12th cent., north door of Church of St. Nicholas, Bari.)

I2: Norman ex-Byzantine mercenary, c. 1085
The fate of large numbers of Normans who had served in Byzantine armies is unknown. So is their equipment, but they are likely to have been issued with Byzantine arms and armour. This is worn by the man shown here. The cuirass of hardened leather scales is a re-interpretation, based upon further study, of a type of armour previously illustrated in MAA125 *The Armies of Islam 7th–11th Centuries*, Plate H1. The helmet has an aventail and a mail hauberk is worn beneath the cuirass. The decorated gaiters are a typical piece of Byzantine cavalry equipment. (Sources: wall painting, late 10th cent., Dovecote Church, Cavusin; *Psalter*, c. 1088, Vatopedi Codex 761, Mt. Athos; helmet, 9th–11th cents., Kazanlak Mus.)

I3: Oshin the Hethoumian, c. 1098
Oshin was the Armenian *stratopedarch* or governor of Cilicia. His polished bronze lamellar cuirass is largely ceremonial, as are the gilded leather splints on his arms. The entire costume is essentially Byzantine, though his small turban and decorated axe are Armenian in style. (Sources: *Adrianople Gospels*, early 11th cent., San Lazzaro Lib., Ms. N.887/116, Venice; wall painting, 11th–12th cents., Balik Kilise, Cappadocia.)

J: The Principality of Antioch:
J1: Knight of Antioch, c. 1268
The last doomed charge by the chivalry of Antioch took place in 1268 against the besieging Mamluk forces. This knight wears the latest European armour with some fashionable differences favoured in the Crusader states. He has a fully developed 'great helm' and perhaps a stiffened leather cuirie or cuirass buckled at the shoulders and worn beneath his surcoat. Iron poleyns have now been added to the padded cuisses over his knees, and he has an early form of basilard dagger on his hip. The horse's caparison is sewn to a heavy felt lining, perhaps with a stiffened leather chamfron to protect the animal's head. (Sources: ceramic fragment from Al Mina, 13th cent., Hatay Mus., Antioch; *Histoire Universelle*, late 13th cent., Bib.Munic., Ms. 562, Dijon and Bib.Nat., Ms.Fr. 20125, Paris, and State Public Lib., Ms.F.v.IV.5, Leningrad.)

J2: Norman-French Crusader, c. 1250–60
After the French conquest of Normandy there seem to have been no differences between Norman military equipment and that of the rest of the country. Here a serjeant wears a chapel-de-fer or war-hat over a padded coif. He is protected by a thick quilted gambeson which includes mittens. His

axe is of a type favoured in northern France and the Low Countries, while his shield bears a red cross on green, a device favoured by French Crusaders. The horse has a full mail bard made in two separate pieces. (Sources: *Maciejowski Bible, c.* 1250, Pierpont Morgan Lib., New York; *Chasse de Sainte Gertrude, c.* 1272, Church of St. Gertrude, Nivelles; *Roman de Toute Chevalerie*, mid-13th cent., Trinity Coll. Lib., Ms. 0.9.34, Cambridge.)

J3: Turcopole, c. 1270
The equipment of the typical Turcopole, if such a 'typical' warrior actually existed, is hard to determine. This man is based on an icon painted in Crusader Palestine, plus other features from French and Byzantine art. (Sources: *St. Sergius*, icon, late 13th cent., St. Catherine's Monastery, Sinai; *History of Outremer*, 1290, Bib.Laur., Ms.Plu. LXI.10, Florence.)

K: Castles and fortifications:
K1: Reconstruction of the 11th-century tower at Mirville
Built early in the 11th century and destroyed by fire around 1100, this tower was the only stone structure in a motte castle which otherwise consisted of a wooden circuit wall and a series of timber buildings.

Late 12th-century capitals showing the mixed equipment of Italo-Norman armies. *Left*, **sleeping guards at the Holy Sepulchre;** *centre*, **a Norman knight—note flower-shaped shield charge;** *right*, **infantrymen, perhaps from North Africa, one with a curved sword.** (*In situ*, **Cloisters, Monreale Cathedral, Sicily**)

It seems to have been typical of small-scale 11th-century fortifications in Normandy.

K2: Reconstruction of the motte of Abinger castle
Only the post-holes of this probably late-11th century wooden tower remain for archaeologists to study. Reconstructions usually show it as a turret raised on stilts, but such a system would have been very vulnerable to fire if an enemy penetrated the outer stockade. Abinger has, therefore, been given here light wattle and daub walling to fill the spaces between the supporting posts.

K3: 12th-century keep of Hedingham Castle
(A) Section showing the biggest Norman arch in England.
(B) Reconstruction showing a wooden entrance ramp which could be removed in an emergency.

Hedingham is the best preserved square keep in England. That of the White Tower in London has been altered, particularly its windows, at a later date.

L: Norman ships:

L1: Mediterranean transport ship, 13th century
Such ships made the expansion and survival of the Crusader states and the Siculo-Norman empire possible. Note the *corridoria* which, replacing an upper deck, were a feature of many Mediterranean 'round ships'.

L2: Norman-French warship, early 13th century
This kind of ship was a development of Viking longships, the warlike dragonship and the more peaceful *knorr*. With castles added fore and aft, it dominated warfare in northern waters for many years.

L3: Siculo-Norman war-galley, late 12th century
The Italian galley was a development of the famous Byzantine *dromon*. The main difference between medieval warships and their classical predecessors was that a ram had been raised above the water-line. Thus it became an oar-smashing, ship-disabling, rather than ship-sinking weapon. This probably reflected the increasing cost of warships as the Mediterranean coasts became deforested.

L4: William the Conqueror's flagship Mora
This picture is taken from the Bayeux Tapestry. It shows a lantern at the flagship's masthead, a monstrous figurehead comparable to those of earlier Viking warships, and a new form of carved sternpost.

L5: Profiles of archetypal 13th-century Mediterranean ships
(A) Three-decker Venetian, which was probably the largest form of 13th-century ship. (B) Four-decker. (C) Two-decker. (D) *Salandrium*, a specialised horse-transport.

'Triumph of Tancred', showing (*top row*) **a miniature royal parasol;** (*middle row*) **Muslim musicians and spearmen;** (*bottom row*) **archers and crossbowmen of various origins. Late 12th–early 13th century Sicilian manuscript.** (*Chronicle of Peter of Eboli*, **Ms.Cod.120/II, Burgerbib., Berne**)

Notes sur les planches en couleur

A1 L'habit de l'évêque comprend un type ancien de mitre, un pallium en forme de T autour des épaules, un manteau ou une chasuble en laine fine en dessous de laquelle on peut voir les glands dorés de la *stola*, et par-dessous encore, le dalmatique et l'aube de lin blanc. **A2** Haubert de style ancien, fendu sur les côtés pour le combat au sol, et bouclier rond de style ancien. A noter les javelots que portait le soldat ainsi que la lance. **A3** Les mercenaires de la Belgique occidentale étaient très recherchés au 11ème siècle. Remarquer un modèle très ancien d'arbalète.

BC1 Armure la plus récente comprenant un casque fait d'une seule pièce, avec le nasal décoré, des manches et des jambières de mailles, et un haubert. On s'interroge beaucoup sur la signification des plaques carrées qui ornent la poitrine des hommes de la Tapisserie de Bayeux; peut-être s'agit-il de ventails de casque non lacés, de sorte que les hommes montrés ici ne semblent pas être au combat; pourtant, les détails des ventails normands restent obscurs. La massue est un symbole d'autorité, non une arme véritable. **BC2** La tapisserie montre Odo dans une armure différente: il s'agit peut-être d'un manteau *jazerant* doublé de mailles et rembourré; son casque et sa masse d'armes attestent une influence méditerranéenne. **BC3** Chevalier typique du nord de la France. Remarquer le casque peint et les lacets du cou, destinés peut-être à serrer la coiffe ou la doublure du casque. **BC4** Certains archers de la tapisserie semblent être des professionnels

Farbtafeln

A1 Das Bischofsgewand umfasst eine frühe Form der *Mitra*; das T-förmige *Pallium* un die Schultern; die *Kasel*, ein Umhang aus feiner Wolle, unter der wir die goldenen Quasten seiner *Stola* sehen; darunter wurde die *Dalmatika* und die *Alba* aus weissen Leinen getragen. **A2** Eine alte Panzer-*Halsberge*, seitlich geschlitzt für den Kampf zu Fuss, und ein alter Rundschild. Man beachte, dass neben der Lanze auch Speere getragen wurden. **A3** Westbelgische Söldner waren im 11. Jahrhundert sehr gesucht; man beachte die sehr alte Form der Armbrust.

BC1 Die neueste Rüstung: einteiliger Helm mit verziertem Nasenschutz, Panzerärmel und Beinteile zusätzlich zur *Halsberge*. Die quadratischen Brustplatten der Männer auf dem Wandteppich von Bayeux sind viel diskutiert worden; wir glauben, dass es sich dabei um geöffnete *Helmvisiere* handelt, weshalb sie hier nicht als von Männern in der Schlacht getragen gezeigt werden; Einzelheiten über normannische *Visiere* sind allerdings nicht bekannt. Die Keule ist ein Symbol der Authorität, keine wirkliche Waffe. **BC2** Der Wandteppich von Bayeux zeigt Odo in einer anderen Rüstung, wahrscheinlich ein mit Kettenhemd gefütterter *Jazerant*mantel; auch sein Helm und Morgenstern zeigen mediterrane Einflüsse. **BC3** Typisch nordfranzösischer Ritter; man beachte den bemalten Helm; und die Schnüre am Hals—vielleicht zum Befestigen der *Helmkappe* und/oder des Helmfutters? **BC4** Manche Bogenschützen auf dem Wandteppich scheinen gut ausgerüstete Berufssoldaten zu sein; andre, einfacher gekleidet,

bien équipés; d'autres, habillés plus simplement, sont probablement des marins de la flotte normande, plutôt que des conscrits d'origine paysanne. **BC5** D'autres sources de 11ème siècle fournissent des renseignements au sujet de ce fantassin professionnel des territoires méridionaux du duc. Le casque rond constitué de deux éléments et le bouclier ovale ont une origine très ancienne. **BC6** Presque indifférenciables des Normands, ces troupes d'élite de la maison de Saxe utilisaient la hache danoise et des boucliers ronds, ovales ou en forme de losange. Certains semblent avoir porté des coiffes de mailles séparées.

D1 Habits aristocratiques flatteurs du 12ème siècle comprenant de larges manches qui révèlent des sous-vêtements en lin à nombreux plis, des robes coupées de façon à souligner la silhouette, et de longues nattes auxquelles on ajoutait souvent des postiches. **D2** Le soupirant de la dame, qui joue du psaltérion, offre un exemple ancien de casques et de boucliers peints de motifs demi-héraldiques. La forme de son casque, incliné vers l'avant, indique probablement une plus grande épaisseur sur le devant. **D3** Vers 1100, les manches des haubertes étaient longues, les jupes plus longues qu'auparavant, et les boucliers étaient devenus énormes. Remarquer le casque à rainures inhabituel, avec une mentonnière attachée directement au rebord.

E1 Remarquer les gants de mailles et les lanières externes, renforcées par des bandes de fer, ajoutées au casque composé d'une seule pièce et au bouclier. Vers cette époque, certains casques furent assortis de masques couvrant le visage, qui devinrent par la suite le 'grand heaume'. **E2** Les casques coniques sont désormais remplacés par des casques ronds. Les boucliers d'infanterie apparurent dans des modèles spécialisés; celui-ci, par exemple, est immense, il s'agit presque d'un mantelet. Les armoiries sont celles du service du Marshal of England. **E3** Certains types de casques à partie supérieure plate sont antérieurs au 'grand heaume' dans certaines régions sous influence scandinave. Le maillotin, associé parfois à un bouclier léger ovoïde, a peut-être servi principalement au 'jugement par combat'.

F1 Le heaume est porté par-dessus un bonnet rembourré. La forme des épaules indique que le soldat portait des vêtements fortement rembourrés et couverts peut-être de cuir rigide. Remarquer également les cuissards. **F2** Ce casque importé atteste une influence étrangère, mais le petit bouclier en cuir et les javelots sont de fabrication locale traditionnelle. **F3** Les porteurs de hache écossais couverts d'une armure servaient de mercenaires en Irlande, où ils faisaient face aux envahisseurs bien équipés. La hache incrustée d'argent est typiquement celte, mais le glaive atteste une influence scandinave continue.

G1 Des influences méridionales firent passer de mode le port d'une armure lourde, et il fut dès lors presque impossible de distinguer les Normands des Italiens et des Byzantins. **G2** On dénotera une très forte influence byzantine ou islamique dans plusieurs sources picturales. Le casque est de caractère fortement oriental et le bouclier à base plate fortement italien. A noter le sabre ancien de cimeterre. **G3** Tir caractéristique, en-dessous du bouclier. Cet archer musulman porte un haubert léger; pourtant, la plupart des soldats musulmans ne portaient pas d'armure.

H1 Remarquer le casque doré par endroits, avec masque, la coiffe de mailles recouverte de tissu et les protections de pieds en armure à écailles, très modernes pour l'époque. **H2** Les articles d'origine balkanique ou byzantine comprennent un type ancien de casque en forme de salade avec couvre-nuque, le sabre-briquet très large et l'arbalète du Moyen-Orient. Remarquer l'empreinte de pied' qui fait saillie. **H3** Portant une armure probablement plus complète que la plupart des conscrits musulmans, ce soldat est armé d'une catapulte.

I1 Ce sergent, qui délivre un message de Tancrède au chef arménien Oshin de Lampron, porte une cuirasse lamellaire de style byzantin caractéristique de l'influence de Byzance sur l'Apulie. **I2** Equipement principalement byzantin porté par ce mercenaire capturé. A noter le haubert sous une cuirasse d'écailles de cuir dur et les guêtres décorées. **I3** La cuirasse de bronze poli et les manches de cuir doré n'étaient généralement portées qu'à l'occasion de cérémonies. Si le costume est en majeure partie byzantin, le turban et la hache, en revanche, sont arméniens.

J1 L'armure européenne la plus récente: 'grand heaume', cuirasse de cuir en dessous du surcot, cuissards rembourrés, genouillères métalliques rembourrées, et poignard *basilard*. Les armures des chevaux sont cousues sur une doublure de feutre, peut-être avec une armure de tête en cuir dur. **J2** Ce cheval porte une protection de mailles composée de deux éléments. Le bouclier est peint de la croix rouge sur fond vert qui affectionnaient les croisés français. Le personnage porte un *chapel-de-fer* par-dessus une coiffe rembourrée, un *gambeson* à l'épaisse doublure, des gants et une hache que l'on trouvait fréquemment dans le nord de la France et les Pays-Bas. **J3** Reconstitué à partir d'une icône peinte en Palestine à l'époque des croisades et d'autres exemples de l'art français et byzantin, il pourrait s'agir ici d'un Turcopole typique, à supposer que ceci ait jamais existé.

K1 Petite fortication normande caractéristique, la tour est la seule construction en pierres, les autres bâtiments et le mur d'enceinte étant faits de bois. **K2** Essai de reconstitution à partir d'éléments présents dans le sol. Nous avons rempli des zones qui séparent les 'surhaussements' favorisés dans d'autres reconstitutions, car ceux-ci nous semblent trop vulnérables aux incendies. **K3** (**A**) Section montrant la plus grande arche normande en Europe; (**B**) Section montrant une rampe d'entrée en bois qui pouvait être retirée en cas d'urgence. Hedingham est le donjon carré le mieux préservé d'Angleterre.

L1 Le bateau dont dépendait l''empire' normand en Méditerranée. Remarquer la *corridoria*, qui remplace le pont supérieur. **L2** Ce bateau de guerre rappelait à la fois le dragon viking et le plus pacifique *knorr*. Avec ses gaillards avant et arrière, il domina la guerre maritime du nord de l'Europe durant des générations. **L3** Navire élaboré à partir du *dromon* byzantin; son éperon est déplacé au-dessus de la ligne de flottaison. **L4** A noter la lanterne en haut du mât, la figure de proue et l'étambot sculpté. **L5** (**A**) Trois-ponts vénitien; (**B**) Quatre-ponts; (**C**) Deux-ponts((**D**) *Salandrium* pour le transport des chevaux.

dürften eher Matrosen der normannischen Flotte als aufgebotene Bauern sein. **BC5** Andere Quellen aus dem 11. Jahrhundert bieten Hinweise für solche Berufsfussoldaten aus den südlichen Gebieten des Herzogs. Der zweiteilige, runde Helm und der ovale Schild sind sehr alt herkunft. **BC6** Fast nicht zu unterscheiden von den Normannen sind diese sächsischen Elite-Haustruppen, die dänische Äxte verwendeten und runde, ovale oder drachenförmige Schilde. Manche dürften separate Panzer*helmkappen* getragen haben.

D1 Die kleidsame aristokratische Mode des 12. Jahrhunderts zeigte weite Ärmel, die die viel gefältelten Leinenunterkleider sehen lassen; Gewänder, deren Schnitt sich gut dem Körper anpasste; und lange Zöpfe, oft durch falsches Haar ergänzt. **D2** Ihr Verehrer spielt auf einem *Psalterium* und zeigt ein frühes Beispiel für das Bemalen von Helmen und Schilden mit semi-heraldischen Mustern. Die nach vorn geneigte Form dieses Helms weist wahrscheinlich auf essen verstärktes Vorderteil hin. **D3** Etwa um 1100 waren die Helmärmel lang, und die Schurze länger als je zuvor; die Schilde waren riesig geworden. Man beachte den ungewöhnlichen, gerillten Helm, mit dem Kinnriemen direkt am Helmrand befestigt.

E1 Man beachte die Panzerfäustlinge; äussere eiserne Verstärkungsbänder zum einteiligen Helm und zum Schild. Um diese Zeit kamen Helme mit Gesichtsmasken auf, die später zum 'grossen Helm' wurden. **E2** Konische Helme wurden nun durch abgerundete Formen ersetzt. Fussvolk-Schilde kamen in spezialisierten Formen auf; dieser hier ist riesig, fast ein *Sturmdach*. Die Wappenzeichen sind die der Dienstleute des Marschalls von England. **E3** Manche Helme mit flacher Glocke gingen in skandinavischen Einflussgebieten dem 'grossen Helm' voraus. Der Striethammer, manchmal in Verbindung mit einem leichten, eiförmigen Schild, dürfte meistens für Zweikämpfe im 'Gottesgericht' verwendet worden sein.

F1 Der Helm wird über einer gepolsterten Helmkappe getragen; die Form der Schultern zeigt stark gepolsterte Kleidungsstücke an, vielleicht sogar aus steifem Leder; man beachte auch den Schenkelschutz. **F2** Ein importierter Helmzeigt äussere Einflüsse, aber der kleine Lederschild und die Speere sind lokale Tradition. **F3** Gepanzerte schottische Axtträger dienten in Irland als Söldner gegen gut ausgerüstete Invasoren. Die mit Silber eingelegte Axt ist typisch keltisch; das Schwert zeigt den fortgesetzten skandinavischen Einfluss.

G1 Südliche Einflüsse führten zum Tragen von etwas weniger Rüstung, und die Normannen waren bald von Italienern und Byzantinern kaum zu unterscheiden. **G2** Byzantinische oder islamische Einflüsse sind in mehreren Bildquellen sehr stark. Der Helm ist sehr östlich, der Schild mit seiner flachen Basis sehr italienisch; man beachte die frühe Form des *Krummschwerts*. **G3** Dieser moslemische Bogenschütze, der auf typische Weise 'unter' seinem Schild hervorschiesst, trägt eine leichte *Halsberge*, die meisten aber kämpften ohne jede Rüstung.

H1 Man beachte den teilweise vergoldeten Helm mit Maske und die gepanzerte, stoffbezogene *Helmkappe*; aber auch den Schuppenpanzer-Fussschutz, sehr modern für jene Zeit. **H2** Zu Stücken balkanescher oder byzantinischer Herkunft gehört der *Schallern*-Helm mit Nackenschutz, das sehr breite Kurzschwert und die nahöstliche Armbrust—man beachte den hervorstehende Fussbalken. **H3** Wahrscheinlich besser gerüstet als die meisten moslemischen Soldaten, ist er mit einer Schleuder bewaffnet.

I1 Dieser *Sergeant*, der dem armenischen Fürsten Oshin von Lampron eine Botschaft von Tankred überbringt, trägt einen Schuppenkürass byzantinischer Art, typisch für den byzantinischen Einfluss in Apulien. **I2** Dieser gefangenen-ommene Söldner trägt hauptsächlich byzantinische Ausrüstung—man beachte die Panzerhalsberge unter dem Kürass aus hartem Schuppenleder, und die verzierten Hosenträger. **I3** Ein polierter Bronze-Kürass mit Armteilen aus vergoldetem Leder ist hauptsächlich für zeremonielle Anlässe gedacht; das Kostüm ist zwar hauptsächlich byzantinisch, Turban und Axt aber sind armenisch.

J1 Die 'modernste' europäische Rüstung: der 'grosse helm'. Leder-Kürass unter dem Überwurf; gepolsterter Schenkel- und eiserner Knieschutz; und der *Basilard*-Dolch. Pferdebeschläge sind auf eine Filzfütterung aufgenäht, vielleicht mit einem Kopfteil aus hartem Leder. **J2** Dieses Pferd hat einen Kettenhemdpanzer in zwei Teilen. Der Schild trägt das rote Kreuz auf grünem Grund nach Muster der französischen Kreuzfahrer. Er trägt einen *Chapel-de-fer* über einer gepolsterten *Helmkappe*, und ein *gefüttertes Wams* mit Fausthandschuhen; und er trägt eine in Nordfrankreich und den Niederlanden beliebte Axt. **J3** Diese Rekonstruktion nach einem Ikon der palästinensischen Kreuzfahrerzeit und anderen französischen und byzantinischen Darstellungen wird mit einigen Zweifeln als 'typischer Türkenpole' angeboten, falls es soetwas je gegeben hat.

K1 Typische kleine normannische Befestigung, mit dem Turm als einziges Steingebilde; Holzgebäude mit umgebendem Wall. **K2** Rekonstruktionsversuch aus überlebenden Relikten; wir haben die Zwischenräume zwischen den Tragpfeilern, die in anderen Rekonstruktionen so beliebt sind, ausgefüllt, weil wir sie für zu anfällig für Feuer hielten. **K3** (**A**) Ein Ausschnitt zeigt den grössten normannischen Bogen in Europa; (**B**) eine hölzerne Eingangsrampe, die bei Gefahr entfernt werden konnte. Hedingham hat den besterhaltenen viereckigen Burgturm in England.

L1 Das Schiff, von dem das ganze normannische 'Empire' im Mittelmeer abhängig wae; man beachte die *Corridoria* anstelle des Oberdecks. **L2** Dieses Kriegsschiff weist zwei Einflüsse auf—die Drachenschiffe der Wikinger und die friedlicheren *Knorr*-Schiffe. Mit seinem Vorder- und Hinterdeck beherrschte dieses Schiff Generationen hindurch die Seekriege Nordeuropas. **L3** Entwickelt aus dem byzantinischen *Dromon*-Schnellsegler, aber mit der Ramme über dem Wasserspiegel. **L4** Man beachte die Laterne am Mast; Gallionsfigur; und der geschnitzte Achtersteven. **L5** (**A**) Venetianer mit drei Decks; (**B**) mit vier Decks; (**C**) mit zwei Decks; (**D**) *Salandrium* zum Pferdetransport.